Antique Recollections

A catalogue record of this book is available from the British Library

First Edition: March 2005

ISBN: 1-84375-149-6

To order additional copies of this book please visit:
http://www.upso.co.uk/barryjones

Published by: UPSO Ltd
5 Stirling Road, Castleham Business Park,
St Leonards-on-Sea, East Sussex TN38 9NW United Kingdom
Tel: 01424 853349 Fax: 0870 191 3991
Email: info@upso.co.uk   Web: http://www.upso.co.uk

To MARTIN

All the Best

(THE BATUM)

Antique Recollections

by

Barry Jones

UPSO

TO SKIPPY AND DAD

WHO SAW IT ALL HAPPEN

PREFACE

There have been many books written about antiques. How to recognise an antique. How much is it worth? etc. But there have been very few books written about the actual antique business itself.

Antique Recollections does just that. It describes the day to day workings of an antique dealer. How he works. Where he obtains his stock, and what finally happens to it.

As well as this, it also recounts the life, the experiences and the growing up of the antique dealer, 'The Bantam', himself.

Antique Recollections exposes a lot of the hitherto unanswered questions about the antiques trade. Secrets that dealers are reluctant to reveal. Who are the knockers? What is meant by a Ring? What is an antique?

In a very humorous and entertaining way it gives the reader a glimpse into the mysterious world of the antique dealer. One full of interest and fascination. As the reader follows the career, and the life of the Bantam. A young man who decided to enter this unknown environment.

In writing this book, my thanks and appreciation go out to, Janet, Narelle and Margaret, whose help and cooperation have been invaluable.

BARRY RICHARD JONES

CONTENTS

Chapter One

Bill's Grandfather Clock

'Five hundred and thirty pounds.'

The auctioneer's eyes rapidly scanned the room. 'Five hundred and thirty pounds, do I have any advance on five hundred and thirty pounds?' and, seeing no further interest he quickly searched the room for a last time, then brought the hammer down with a deafening bang. 'Sold to Mr Evans,' he said, a smile creeping upon his face. Behind him, stood Mr Evans, a small weasel faced little man about fifty years of age with almost no hair on his head and a pair of brass rimmed glasses perched precariously on the end of his nose. His speciality was Longcase clocks and he was writing furiously into his little red book, his thin lips parted in a smirk of satisfaction.

Brian Richards, known in the antiques trade as The Bantam just couldn't believe it. Five hundred and thirty pounds! He couldn't get over it, five hundred and thirty pounds for a horrible, fat, late nineteenth century mahogany grandfather clock. That was incredible, an amazing price for a clock of that calibre. Its painted dial showed the movements of the moon, and tides, whilst on either side of the case were a pair of large, fat barley sugar twist pillars with a smaller matching pair on the hood. To his mind, of all the grandfather clocks he had ever had through his hands, the Yorkshire grandfather clock had to rate as the ugliest of them all, Mr Evans' being of no exception.

Later, watching Mr Evans as he carefully detached the hood, and removed the pendulum from the eight day movement (making certain not to snap the thin metal feather at the top), Brian cast his mind back a few years, to the first Yorkshire clock that he had ever bought, and a smile crossed his face.

That was in the days when antique dealing was a lot of fun and antiques were more plentiful, the Bantam mused to himself, as he slowly made his way out of the auction room. Unfortunately, the fun had now gone out of the business and it was all dog eat dog today.

In the old days, Brian reminisced, as he slowly drove his bright orange Volvo estate out of the car park, when you bought a piece of furniture from a dealer, there was usually a profit left in it. Unlike now when prices have gone through the roof, and everybody is after the very last penny.

The particular clock that he was actually thinking about had belonged to his soon to be brother-in-law Bill, who, as it transpired, not long after turned out to be his ex brother-in-law.

Brian had only been in the antique trade for a short while, having left the Royal Air Force six months previously, at the tender age of twenty. He had joined up at the age of seventeen (much against his mother's wishes), and after trade training had been sent out to North Africa where he stayed living under canvas for two years, an experience that stayed with him for the rest of his life.

Always the smallest in his class at school, he had grown into a thin pale faced young man with blue eyes and fair hair, standing about five feet eight inches tall and weighing about nine stone, and it was to be a few years before he filled out and became a bigger, stronger and very much wiser person, but what he lacked in brawn, however, he made up for in brains.

Being an avid reader, and having plenty of spare time, he had read a lot about antiques and decided that he would go into the antiques trade on his demob from the Air Force.

Unfortunately Brian was a very self-centred, selfish person, who had little or no thought for others, which was how he came to be known as The Bantam. He thought that it was the name of a chicken, and it was years later before he finally found out that the nickname was given to him because of his attitude towards his fellow men, not because of his size.

He had been in the antiques trade for only a few months, but was already beginning to find his feet. He was gaining confidence in himself and his ability to buy antiques, and found he took to it as readily as a duck takes to water.

However, there is only one way to learn the antiques trade, and that is to put your money where your mouth is. It is one thing to say 'I think that chest of drawers is worth fifty pounds', but it is quite another to buy it and then go out and try to make a profit on it. Only time and experience can teach you the business. Books can give you a rough idea on the prices involved, but an antique is only worth what someone is prepared to pay for it, the Bantam soon realised, and different people have different views on that subject, as he was to find out in the years to come.

Bill, Brian's brother-in-law, was an ex sea captain, at least that's what he said, but Brian had his doubts. It must be admitted that he certainly looked the part. He stood about five feet ten inches tall with broad shoulders, and a jovial, weather beaten face that looked well lived in. He must have been about fifty years old, and his greying hair and beard reminded Brian somewhat of the Captain Birds Eye advert on the television. Nevertheless he was a nice enough chap, even if he was inclined to be a bit pompous. If his sister and Bill wished to get married, good luck to them. Brian really wasn't concerned one way or the other.

Bill had had the good fortune to inherit a beautiful seventeenth century cottage and its contents, from the death of a distant aunt that he barely remembered. He, being the sole remaining member of the family, inherited the lot, including the longcase clock. It stood proudly in the corner of his lounge, its carved horns almost touching the roof. The Spanish mahogany case gleamed in the light that came from the crystal chandelier that hung from the oak beamed ceiling, and the slow ticking of the clock, brought a quiet serenity into the room as if it were trying to slow down the mad race of time.

The dial was a masterpiece of Victorian art. Hand painted roses and flowers surrounded it, whilst a full masted schooner rose and fell in the turbulent sea. Each tick of the clock sent it alternately up and down through the white capped waves that were painted upon the arch of the dial.

Made in about 1880 it was a good example of the decline of Victorian furniture. As the nineteenth century drew to its close, grandfather clocks (or Longcase clocks to give them their proper name) became bigger, fatter and uglier as in fact did the rest of the Victorian furniture. Bill's clock being no exception.

But, for all that, it was a Victorian grandfather clock, and if it was at all possible, Brian was going to acquire it one way or another.

The problem was that there was no way that Bill would part with Aunt Bessie's clock. 'It's a family heirloom,' he would proudly boast, which was a bit pretentious of him as he hadn't been aware that he had an Aunt Bessie until he heard from his lawyers that she had left this mortal coil. To hear him talk, one would think that Henry Weaverham of Wetherby had made the clock especially for a distant relative, and that it had been passed on through the family ever since.

But Brian was determined to own it, and a few weeks later, fate gave him the opportunity. Bill and Brian's sister, Mary, had decided that it was time that they finally got married. True to tradition, Bill was determined to have a good boozy stag night down at the Red Lion, which by good fortune, was only situated about a mile down the lane from the cottage.

The Red Lion was an American's dream of a country pub. It had old oak beams, a big log fire, horse brasses on the wall, even the country locals sitting on old pine settles set into the inglenook fireplace, discussing local gossip and drinking bitter straight from the wood. It was a far cry from the chrome and plastic gin palace that today's Red Lion has turned into, with its locals from the new housing estate built where the fields used to be, and the bitter, cold and tasteless out of aluminium kegs.

It was early December, and the winter was starting to set in. The sky held the promise of the snow to come, and the wind whistled around the Bantam's ears, making them tingle with the cold, as he pushed open the heavy oak studded door of the Red Lion and made his way through the welcoming warmth into the snug.

Bill was in his usual place, perched on a high stool at the corner of the bar surrounded by all his cronies, a glass of malt whiskey clutched in his hand. He was bragging in a loud voice about a deal he had just completed down at the local market.

'Oh God,' Brian groaned to himself, 'he's off again, always boasting and trying to be top dog. One day someone will take him down a peg or two, and with a bit of luck it will be me!'

'Bantam!' Bill cried, as Brian pushed his way through to the bar. He put his arm around the Bantam's shoulder and breathed whiskey fumes into his face. 'What are you going to have old boy? Gentlemen!' he cried, a big grin on his face as he embraced the assembled crowd with a broad sweep of his arm, 'this is the one and only Bantam, my brother-in-law to be. He's in antiques, although God knows why, he doesn't know a thing about them, but he's learning. Aren't you old chap?' He squeezed Brian's arm painfully and gave him a slow cynical wink. 'What are you having my son? Whiskey is it?'

'Just half please, Bill,' Brian answered slowly, an idea beginning to germinate in his head. 'Just a half.'

A few moments later a half pint glass was thrust into his hand, and being in deep thought, he unconsciously raised it to his lips and took a deep swallow. It nearly choked him, as he realised too late that what he had been given was half a pint of whiskey, instead of the half of lager that he had expected. Everybody roared with laughter.

'Well old son,' yelled Bill, 'you did say a half!' He chortled and everybody fell about as Brian choked and spluttered on his drink, doing his best not to make a fool of himself.

The evening roared on and the drinks flowed freely. The Bantam, the butt of someone else's joke yet again, said nothing but quietly bided his time. He was more determined than ever to take possession of Auntie Bessie's clock, and to get one up on Bill.

Firstly, he had to get into Bill's workshop, which wouldn't be difficult, as it wasn't locked. Most of all, he had to get to the cottage before everybody else. Even now, Bill was drunkenly insisting in a loud voice that the party should adjourn back to the cottage. So if the deed was to be done Brian had to do it quickly.

He picked his way carefully through the crowd to the bar, and in a loud voice called to the barman, 'Hey Sam, can we have one for the road?' As Sam the barman began to compile the order, Brian surreptitiously pocketed a dart from the half dozen or so that were standing in a pint pot on the bar. No one had noticed what he had done, and he grinned to himself in anticipation. Part one had gone according to plan, now for part two of Operation Auntie Bessie!

He slowly turned to Bill, a smile on his face. 'Hey Bill,' he said, putting his arm affectionately around the older man's shoulder, 'why don't you give me the key to the cottage and whilst you lot are finishing off your drinks, I'll go and light the fire and get things set up before you get back. What do you think? It will save a bit of time won't it?

'Good idea mate,' murmured Bill, as he handed over an old heavy wrought iron key that must have been as old as the cottage itself. 'You go ahead and get things set up,' and he buried his nose back into his glass of whiskey.

Smiling quietly to himself at the success of his plan, Brian thrust the key into his pocket and made his way out into the cold night. The snow as just starting to fall as he walked quickly down the lane towards the cottage. He didn't have much time to do what he had in mind, but things were working out in his favour. It is said that the Devil looks after his own, and he was certainly looking after his own this night! If he hurried, he could get into Bill's workshop, do what was necessary, and light the fire in the lounge before the rest o them got back from the pub.

The clock stood like a sentinel in the corner of the lounge as Brian pushed open the heavy oak door of the cottage and brushed the snow from his coat. As he quickly lit the fire, which had already been laid, the flickering flames reflected in the polished mahogany case of the old clock, as the schooner still ploughed its way remorsefully across the rolling fiery sea. The ticking of the heavy pendulum permeated through the oak beamed lounge, giving it a quiet peaceful atmosphere as Brian, the grin still on his face, commenced Operation Auntie Bessie! To hell with Bill he thought, as he helped himself to a large glass of his brother-in-law's whiskey, Aunt Bessie's clock was going to be his!

He had just got everything finished in time, as Bill, cursing the weather outside, drunkenly pushed open the heavy oak door, and staggered in, along with the rest of the party. 'Christ, it's bitter outside,' he complained, as he brushed the snow to the floor, rubbing his hands briskly together and standing in front of the, now blazing, log fire. 'Let's have a drink to warm us up. What are you going to have Bant?'

As the party continued, Brian slowly turned the subject of the conversation to antiques. 'You're not too keen on antiques are you Bill?' he said quietly as he thrust another glass of whiskey into Bill's greedy outstretched hand.

'Of course I am,' Bill retorted, taking a long swallow of the drink, and banging the glass down on a glass topped coffee table at his side with such force that Brian thought he would break the glass. 'But when all is said and done, antiques are nothing special. They're only commodities to be bought and sold like anything else. As you should know, Bant, it's your business.'

'Maybe, Bill,' replied Brian, pouring another generous measure of whiskey into Bill's now empty glass, his thoughts racing ahead, 'maybe they are, but if you had any antiques you wouldn't part with them would you? Take that clock for instance,' he continued, turning to Auntie Bessie's clock, 'there's no way that you'd part with that would you?' A broad smile on his face.

By this time, the rest of the crowd were beginning to take an interest in the conversation. It's a strange thing, Brian thought as he smiled to himself, but as soon as a conversation turns to antiques, people stop and listen. Maybe it's because to most people antiques are a mysterious subject and they want to know more about them. Whatever the reason, it seems to draw a crowd like bees to a honey pot, and this suited the Bantam's purpose perfectly.

'What's it worth Bill?' cried a voice from across the room.

'Yes Bill,' said Brian, a large grin splitting his face, 'what do you reckon the clock is worth?' He crossed his fingers and waited for the reply, on which his whole plan rested.

Bill sat thoughtfully for a moment, his expression one of deep thought. 'Well I reckon that it's worth forty of fifty pounds of anybody's money, don't you?' Bill laughed loudly as he looked around the room at the interested faces that were watching the drama unfold. 'It's got to be worth that, or my name's not Bill Edwards,' and he took another large gulp of his drink.

Brian smiled to himself, things were going better than he had hoped. 'I'll tell you what Bill,' he said, standing up and walking across to the clock. 'I'll give you a hundred pounds for it now cash in your hand,' and he put his hand in his pocket.

The room went suddenly quiet. All that could be heard was the tick tock of the clock in the corner. A voice whispered, 'He's bloody crazy, there's no way it's worth that much.' Bill sat staring up from the depths of his high backed leather chair, a look of amazement on his face, his now forgotten glass of whiskey still clutched in his hand.

Time seemed to stand still as the Bantam held his breath and waited. Everything he had planned depended on Bill's answer. If there was one thing that he had learnt in his short life, it is that people are greedy and everyone loves a bargain, and Bill was no exception.

Brian was far from being stupid. He knew a lot about people and the way that they act and think. At the same time he also had a streak of honesty running through him and would never have deliberately stolen from anybody. Indeed he was always a sucker for a hard luck story, and would help anybody out. But if someone allowed themselves to be hoodwinked by their own greed, in Brian's eyes that was all right.

As he watched the look of astonishment cross Bill's face, he had no qualms about what was about to happen.

Bill, in his view, deserved it, and the Bantam knew that Operation Auntie Bessie was going to be a success and that his assessment of Bill's character was correct.

'How much did you say?' Bill said taking a slow sip of the diminishing contents of his glass. 'Did you say a hundred quid?' A thoughtful look crossing his craggy face.

'Yes,' smiled Brian, pulling a large roll of one pound notes out of his pocket. He had made them all one pound notes to make the roll look purposely bigger, because he knew what Bill's reaction would be.

Bill's eyes lit up. 'It's a deal!' he cried, jumping out of his chair, knocking his glass to the floor in his excitement. 'For a hundred quid, you can have the bloody thing, you're the antique dealer, you're the expert. Who am I to argue with you?' He held out his hands for the roll of notes, his face alive with anticipation, his eyes full of greed.

'By the way Bill,' murmured Brian quietly, taking a sip of his own drink, 'I trust that there's no woodworm in the clock!'

'Woodworm!' Bill exclaimed, looking at him with fire in his eyes, 'Woodworm!' His voice rose an octave. 'Of course there's no bloody woodworm in it! Why should there be woodworm in the damn thing?'

At this, the rest of the company excitedly started to examine the clock. 'Hey Bant,' cried a voice, 'how do you tell it it's got worm?'

Brian turned slowly, picked up his glass trying hard not to give way to the nervous tension that was threatening to show itself. 'There will be little holes about the size of a pin head,' he replied slowly, 'and if it's live, you should see signs of wood dust on the floor.' He turned to face Bill, who by now was showing distinct signs of anxiety. 'Bill' he said quietly 'if it has got worm, you have got a lot of problems.'

'How come, what problems will I have?' asked Bill.

'Well if it has,' Brian replied, looking him straight in the eyes, 'it will spread into the floorboards and from there into the beams and structure of the cottage. Once woodworm starts, there is no stopping it.'

What he omitted to tell Bill was that woodworm is only active for three months of the year, April, May and June. This being December, no woodworm in his right mind would show his face outside the confines of this Victorian masterpiece.

At that moment, a cry came from behind the clock, 'Hey Bill take a look at this!'

'Damn' yelled Bill, and sprung towards the clock, a look of horror on his face. 'I don't believe it, I just don't believe it!' He knelt by the side of the clock, looking despairingly at the dozen or so small holes that were in it and fingering the fine dust that lay on the carpet. 'What do I do now?' he wailed, 'it's full of bloody worm.'

'If I were you old son,' Brian said smoothly, 'I would get rid of it fast, but don't look at me, there's no way I would pay one hundred pounds for a clock full of worms.'

The disappointment on Bill's face was a picture, as he saw his hundred pounds disappearing like water soaked up by the sand, and he didn't like it one little bit.

'I'll tell you what,' Brian went on quickly 'I will give you forty pounds for it. I must be mad, the condition that it's in, but what the heck, you are almost my brother-in-law, and I might be able to do something with it,' and he counted forty pound notes into his hand.

Bill quickly snatched the forty pounds from Brian's

outstretched hand, and shoved it quickly into his pocket. 'It's a deal,' he cried, 'you have bought the clock for forty pounds, and there are witnesses to prove it. Right lads?' And he turned to face his friends, who by now were convinced that Brian had gone quite out of his mind.

'Don't worry Bill,' Brian retorted, a large grin on his face as he emptied his glass, and made a mental note to return the dart to the bar of the Red Lion before it was missed. 'As you say, I don't know about antiques.' He slowly started to dismantle the clock, wondering as he did so if he had remembered to close the door of Bill's workshop.

Later, as he drove home, Auntie Bessie's clock snugly nestling in the back of the Volvo, Brian felt quite pleased with himself.

The snow was now beginning to fall quite heavily, and he drove carefully, a smug smile on his face, feeling at peace with the world. Happy that he had got one over on Bill.

He wouldn't have felt so peaceful and happy if he had only known what the world was to throw at him before very long.

But he would learn.

Eventually.

Chapter Two

The Dresser

It must have been about six months after the incident of Bill's grandfather clock that Brian met Alice. It must be said that he hadn't had a lot of experience with the opposite sex and he was a little uncertain how to treat them, but Alice he fell for, hook line and sinker.

She was a year younger than him, a pretty girl, about five feet four inches tall, with a full shapely figure, long jet black hair and deep green eyes that fascinated him. In years to come he was to tell Alice that her eyes were like a Jersey cow's, which didn't please her very much, but he meant it in the nicest way because he had always thought that Jersey cows had lovely limpid eyes.

They met one day, by chance, at an antique Sale. Brian was buying stock and Alice was trying to find a bargain to put into her small upstairs flat which she shared with an old tom cat called Fred. Brian found Alice fascinating, and was quite taken with her.

They got along like a house on fire as they both had an interest in antiques and old furniture, and, later, as he left the sale Brian had arranged to meet her the following evening.

But, bright and early next morning, before Brian had hardly had time for breakfast, his thoughts still on his forthcoming meeting with Alice, Danny the Liar arrived with an old Welsh dresser that looked as if it had seen better days. It was perched on the long roof rack that stretched the length of a canary yellow, brand new, Volvo estate car, looking for all the world like a koala bear being carried on the back of its mother.

Beneath the ancient layers of flaking white paint the dark oak timber peered through here and there, like patches of blue in a cloud-filled sky. In parts the back of the rack had been broken away, and woodworm had begun to chew its way relentlessly through the leg of the base. It looked very sad and sorry for itself but Brian knew that he was going to buy it, even before Danny the Liar had untied the rope that held it to the rack. He knew that it was going to be his, he could see beneath the layers of paint and grime to the potential that was waiting to be released.

Danny the Liar, so called because of his complete inability to tell the truth, was one of the knockers; a band of unscrupulous itinerant Irishmen who scoured the countryside knocking on doors to obtain, by any means at their disposal, antiques and works of art. Most of the knockers were dirty and scruffy, but some of them would dress very smartly and go around the churches and convents in their search for antiques. They were deeply religious themselves, their cars and vans were full of religious artefacts and miniature statues of the Virgin Mary. The Bantam often used to wonder how they came to terms with their consciences. They must have had to do an awful lot of confessing, he thought to himself as he helped Danny undo the knots that secured the dresser to the rack.

Unfortunately the days of the knockers are over now. They did such a good job of finding the furniture, and bringing it onto the market that the source of supply has dried up. People are far more aware these days of the value of the things that they own, due to the efforts of television and radio. A few years ago things were different. A lot of dealers made a lot of money from buying from the knockers. The furniture was there for the taking, and take it they did, by fair means or foul.

The methods they used were wrong, but they did at least ensure that a steady supply of furniture became available. One only has to look around to see how many antiques dealers have left the business since the Irishmen ceased their dubious dealings.

One of their favourite tricks was to go into a house and pick on a valueless piece of furniture, a sideboard for instance. If for argument's sake, it was worth fifty pounds they would offer to buy it for three hundred pounds, taking, as they did so, a large wad of notes from their pockets. The unsuspecting owner of the sideboard would be overjoyed at his good fortune. The knockers would then go through the house buying all the antiques in sight. Furniture, copper, brass, paintings etc all at a low price, whilst the owner was still recovering from the shock of selling his sideboard for three hundred pounds.

The sting came when they came to pay out. They would pay for everything except the sideboard saying, 'Sorry love, we can't get the sideboard on the van, we are full up, okay if we pick it up in the morning?' The unsuspecting owner, although being disappointed at not being paid for the sideboard, was still happy in the belief that he had sold all his antiques at a fair price, and would receive the ultimate price for his sideboard the next morning. Needless to say, the knockers never returned.

It is ironic that over the years, the price of antiques having risen so dramatically, that same sideboard is probably now worth a hundred and fifty pounds. But should an antiques dealer, offer a hundred and fifty pounds for it, the owner would think he was trying to cheat him because a few years ago an Irish knocker had offered him a crazy price for it. One only has to ask, 'Was it an Irishman?' to learn the truth.

There must be hundreds of people around the country that dearly cherish their pieces of furniture that the knockers bid on, happy in the belief that they are worth a lot more than they actually are.

Danny slowly climbed out from behind the wheel of the Volvo, a broad smile across his unshaven face, a cigarette smouldering in his mouth, his eyes alight with the battle of wits that was to come. Because buying from the Irishmen was indeed a battle of wits, it was a battle to the end, with no holds barred, and Danny the Liar was an expert in the art of dealing. As in fact were all the Irishmen.

What they didn't know about antiques just wasn't worth knowing, and in the art of wheeling and dealing they had no equal. Learning to buy from the knockers could cost an unsuspecting dealer a great deal of money, as in fact it had cost Brian, but after a few years in the business he felt confident enough to take on any of them.

To look at Danny you would think that he hadn't two pennies to rub together. He was about six feet tall, with a mass of black, unkempt, greasy hair. He hat not shaved for about a week, and smelled as if he had not washed for even longer.

He was dressed in a pair of scruffy old grey flannels, with a patch on one knee, a dirty black jacket covered his broad frame and an old white silk scarf was strung around his neck. But in spite of his scruffy appearance Brian knew that his pockets were full to bursting with large wads of notes, and that the brand new Volvo estate was certainly not bought on hire purchase.

Danny the Liar lived in a large luxurious caravan. It was a palace of plate glass and chrome worth thousands of pounds. Every time that the knockers set up camp they covered all the flat surfaces with Crown Derby china, the status symbol of a successful dealer. The amount he owned denoted his wealth. They had no use for banks or building societies. Crown Derby was their bank.

Most of these people came from the same small village in Southern Ireland, and were nearly all related in some way or other. Back in Ireland they all owned large houses which were full of the best of the furniture and bric-a-brac that they had obtained over the years and regularly taken back home. Inlaid mahogany being their favourite.

'Bantam my old friend,' Danny smiled showing a mouthful of decaying teeth. 'How are you this fine morning? Come and have a look at what I have brought you,' as he fumbled with the ropes holding the dresser to the rack.

'Hold on Danny,' murmured the Bantam, casting a quick eye over the dresser. 'How much is it before you get it off?'

'Now, Banty,' Danny retorted – he always called Brian 'Banty' and it infuriated Brian no end, - 'how can you be asking how much it is when you haven't even had a good look at it?' A large grin split his face and he gave Brian a broad wink.

The Bantam gave a little sigh to himself. The battle had commenced. All he had to do now was to fix a price in his mind and stick to it. That was easier said than done. The haggling and bartering took the best of half an hour, and while the dresser had cost Brian a little more than he had wanted to pay, he was quite happy at the outcome.

On inspection, the dresser was made up. That is to say, instead of being an 18th century oak dresser made in Anglesey, with drawers across the top, cupboards on either side and a set of dummy drawers down the middle, it was in fact a Yorkshire dresser that had fallen into bad repair and had been added to, to give the appearance of an Anglesey dresser. The rack was completely original, but unfortunately the base left a lot to be desired. It had been painted white to hide the mistakes and, with what to Brian was an absolute give away, there was a marked difference in the colours of the oak that had been used in the construction.

Early oak was always slab cut, that is to say, cut along the grain in a saw pit. Two men, one on the top and the other at the bottom of the pit, cut through the whole tree with a large hand saw, the man at the bottom getting covered with shavings, hence the expression the 'underdog'. In later years when sawing was mechanised oak was cut across the grain, which gave it the distinctive modullary rays, and was lighter in colour as it was not as old as the slab cut style. Oak gets blacker as it gets older, and the experienced eye can tell the age of a piece of furniture just by looking at the colour of the wood. One only had to smell a piece of early cut oak to see how old it was.

This didn't present any great problems to Brian, he knew that it would have to be stripped, all the white paint removed, then it would have to be coloured and polished to make it all the same colour, if it was going to pass as an 18th century dresser. Any antique dealer worth his salt would know what it was, but it would be saleable and it would give him a lot of pleasure to restore it.

The Bantam's thoughts went to Alice and the forthcoming evening ahead. He wondered what she would have thought about the dresser, or Danny himself for that matter. What would she think of him paying out a lot of money for what to the layman would look like a load of old rubbish, and he smiled to himself as he helped Danny carry the dresser into the workshop. As things turned out, Alice had a very good aptitude for antiques and, like the Bantam, was able to see the potential in an abused or misused piece of furniture.

The white dresser had cost him fifty pounds, or to be precise, forty eight pounds and two pounds for good luck. Had Brian said fifty pounds without the luck money he would not have been able to buy it. Luck money was important to the Irish, they were a strange people to deal with, and luck money was an important part of any deal. But honour had been satisfied, and as Brian watched the dirty unkempt Irishman climb behind the wheel of the Volvo, he wondered again at the way of life that these strange people led, and the way that they made their living.

In their own way the knockers held a great deal of respect for their fellow men. Turn your back and they would steal from you, weaken in a deal and they would rob you blind and laugh as they were doing it. Conversely if the Bantam had a financial problem Danny the Liar would have put his hand in his pocket and given him as much as he required without a moment's compunction.

Brian well remembered the first visit that he had paid to the knockers' camp. He had just taken possession of a brand new orange Volvo estate, a vehicle much loved by the antiques trade for its ability to carry heavy loads, and he was as proud as punch with the first brand new car that he had ever owned in his life.

As Brian drove into the untidy camp site taking cre to avoid the multitude of scruffy children that ran around the site without a care in the world, he wondered again at the knockers' strange nomadic lifestyle. They just wandered the country, with their palatial caravans, stopping anywhere that they pleased, irrespective of whose land it was, be it private or council, calling on local houses to buy scrap metal or antique furniture. When they had sucked the area dry they would move on to pastures new leaving the camp site left looking like the local refuse tip that had been hit by a bomb.

They paid no taxes, no road tax on their vehicles, or anything else for that matter, and gave not a fig for anyone except their own kind. After they had passed by, the local councils would block the site with loads of rock or gravel to prevent them coming again. The local farmers would heave a sigh of relief, and repair broken fences and pray that they never returned, and the local pub owners would gleefully count their profits.

Brian parked the Volvo carefully next to George the First's caravan. George was so called because everything he sold was supposedly made in the reign of George the First. But needless to say it was usually an assortment of furniture from Edwardian upwards. Although, Brian thought to himself as he climbed out of the Volvo and mentally prepared himself for the forthcoming battle of wits, to be fair, George did occasionally have the occasional piece of nice Georgian furniture. The Bantam stepped into George's beautiful caravan not realising that he had just made one fatal mistake: he had omitted to lock the door of the Volvo!

When he returned about half an hour later after successfully buying some brass lamps, he was dismayed to find that the knockers' children had filled the car with about twenty five of the smelliest, dirtiest dogs that he had ever seen, and were all standing round the vehicle laughing like mad, as the animals barked and fought to get out, climbing all over the interior of Brian's beloved car. The Bantam was not amused. He was very proud of his new Volvo and to see it in this condition made him see red. As he slowly drove home, he cursed the knockers and their scruffy, illiterate children. It took him about a week to get rid of the stench that had permeated into every corner of the vehicle, and some of the scratches were never removed, serving as a reminder to him to always be prepared for the unexpected when dealing with the knockers.

When he told Alice she laughed, until she saw his face and realised that he did not find it funny. 'I'm sorry darling,' she said as she kissed him lightly on the cheek, 'but it does sound rather funny.'

With a rueful grin he had to agree. 'I'll get them back for that,' he vowed, 'just you wait and see.'

It took him about a week of hard work to finish the dresser, until finally it stood in the corner of the workshop in all its glory, the white paint removed, the wood coloured to match, and gleaming with the coats of wax polish that he had applied. To him it was wrong whatever he did to it, it was still a made up dresser. But although he said it himself, it did look the part. As he reviewed his handiwork with pride he felt contented. Anyone not versed in antiques would take it for a genuine eighteenth century oak Anglesey dresser, and he grinned as he gave it a final polish.

It was not long before he sold the dresser to a dealer from down south who called on his monthly buying trip. The dealer knew that it was a made up piece of furniture but, like Brian, he thought he could make a profit with it, and as he loaded it on top of his Volvo and drove slowly down the drive, Brian thought that he had seen the last of the dresser …

It was about a year later that Fate played her card. Brian and Alice had finally decided to get married and accordingly in typical Bantam style, it was done almost immediately.

Brian was very very happy. He had never before experienced the sort of feeling that he felt for Alice and he didn't want to lose it. He found it a good feeling to have someone else to care for and to be loved in return. He was at last beginning to realise that the world didn't revolve completely around himself. He was growing up – finally – and infinitely slowly, he was beginning to mature into a caring person.

It so happened that Brian had a dealer friend who ran an antique shop in Malibu Beach, California, and he wanted him to go over to America and organise a shipment of antiques. It was too good an opportunity to miss. Brian decided that Alice and he would get married as soon as possible and go to America on their honeymoon, an idea that Alice welcomed with open arms.

They had a ball. They took a train from New York to Kansas City, where they stopped for a few days with some dealers who they had met in England when they were over on a buying trip. Alice couldn't get away quickly enough though, because the daughter of the family, although she was only twenty five years old, was already on her third husband. The tall, attractive, long blonde haired beauty was already making eyes at the Bantam and Alice wasn't having any of it. She was already annoyed at the fact that they had to spend the first few days of their honeymoon in bunk beds, this being the only sleeping arrangement in the small compartment that they had booked on the train. Brian was not in the slightest bit put out – he thought it was hilarious.

They spent most of the time in the dining compartment, sitting at the long bar that stretched halfway down the carriage, and admiring the beauty of the American countryside as it passed quickly by. As she gazed out of the window and sipped her drink, Alice murmured, musing out loud 'Why me? Why am I so lucky?' but the Bantam didn't hear her, his thoughts were in California and the business that was to come.

From Kansas City they took a Greyhound bus to California, stopping at Las Vegas and Reno on the way and eventually they arrived in Los Angeles. They found themselves a very comfortable, reasonably priced hotel, and thankfully booked themselves in for a couple of days.

Alice was shattered, 'I'm going for a sleep my love – are you coming?' and she held her arms out invitingly. 'Not yet, Pet,' Brian kissed Alice on the forehead, 'I'm too hyped up, I'm going to go for a walk,' and he made his way out of the hotel leaving Alice with a look of disappointment on her face. It was a boiling hot day and the temperature was climbing relentlessly into the nineties. The perspiration was dripping off the Bantam and he was feeling very hot, sticky and tired. He couldn't wait to get back to the hotel and have a cool shower and an even cooler beer.

He strolled slowly down the streets, past high class shops and fashion shops, winding his way through the crowds of midday shoppers. Suddenly he stopped in his tracks dumbfounded. A young woman cannoned into him, dropping her packages and cursing him wildly in a broad southern accent as they cascaded to the ground. Muttering profuse apologies he helped her to retain her packages and turned to look back into the window of the large prosperous looking antique shop behind him.

He had not been mistaken, there it was! The dresser! The same white painted dresser that he had bought from Danny the Liar for fifty pounds over a year ago was now sitting resplendent in the window of an antique shop in downtown Los Angeles. The gilt on the black ticket read 'Genuine Welsh Oak Dresser – circa 1780. $2,500.'

The Bantam stood in unbelievable amazement, completely oblivious to the crowds around him. At the current exchange rate that was an incredible twelve hundred pounds! Some poor unsuspecting American was going to part with two thousand five hundred dollars in the belief that they would own a genuine eighteenth century dresser. Instead of which, they had a made up, bodged piece of junk that wasn't worth a tenth of the price.

Brian chuckled to himself as he resumed his journey back to the hotel. Strange indeed are the ways of the antique world. If only Joe Public knew half of what went on behind the scenes, it would open his eyes.

When he told Alice what he had seen, she made him take her back to the city to the antique shop to see for herself, and like the Bantam, she thought it unbelievable.

'You couldn't get anything more amazing than that now, could you love,' she said as she slipped her arm through Brian's, causing a nice feeling of being wanted to creep over him in a warm glow.

'No, darling, I don't think you could,' he replied with a smile, and turning round to the shop window in which the dresser stood in all its glory, he put his arm lovingly around her shoulder and squeezed her gently.

'Unless, of course, you take into account the fact that the dresser is here in Los Angeles and here we are too, as man and wife. That to my mind is truly amazing, don't you agree?' And hugging each other with glee, they both laughed out loud, causing a few heads to turn in surprise, as they made their way back to the hotel still laughing hilariously.

Chapter Three

The Donkey Box

On his return from America, Brian decided that it was high time that he had an antique shop of his own. It was all very well selling to the trade, he thought, but by selling retail, it was possible to get just that little bit extra.

It would also be good for buying in stock and obtaining house clearances. So he made an arbitrary decision. He would find a shop. Alice was overjoyed with the idea. So much so, that, as soon as Brian broached the idea, she insisted that they went out immediately to have a look around and see what they could find.

As luck would have it, within the next few days they found just what they were looking for. It was a shop with a flat above, that were perfectly suited to their requirements. It was situated on a main road and had space at the back for storage and a workshop.

For once in his life, the Bantam had made the right decision.

It was about six weeks after they had seen the white dresser in America, that Jack Cummins, the Bantam's friend from Malibu Beach, arrived in England. He had come over to purchase enough furniture and bric-a-brac to fill a forty foot container and Brian had agreed to run him around to look for furniture, pack the container, and generally take care of things at this end. He was going to pay Brian for doing all this, and as he had already bought a lot of furniture from him, Brian was well content with the arrangement.

When you realise a forty foot container will take approximately a hundred and fifty items of furniture and heaven knows how many pieces of bric-a-brac, you can understand the enormity of the task that lay before him. But Brian had done it many times before and it held no fears for him.

Jack had a successful antique business in America. Now he was going to expand into the import business, and had come to the Bantam for his assistance. For his part, Brian was only too happy to have a regular customer to send his goods to and they were both hoping the arrangement would work out satisfactorily, which as time would prove, it did.

Jack was a colourful character, about five feet ten inches tall, with a thin body and gaunt face. He was about fifty years old and his blonde hair was slowly receding. He wore the American badge of office, plaid slacks, sweater and sneakers, and the inevitable can of Coke was always in his hand. Brian dreaded to think what Jack's insides must have been like, with the amount of Coke that he drank.

Jack Cummins was what was thought of in England as the typical American, loud mouthed, brash and bombastic, but Brian liked him for all that, and they got on well together. He called him JC which tickled Jack immensely. He was staying with Brian and Alice to save the expense of a hotel and he turned out to be the perfect guest.

One evening as they were all sitting down to dinner they decided to go and see a dealer who lived about fifty miles away. It was nine o'clock in the evening and Jack expressed a desire to go straight away rather than wait until the following day. Brian telephoned to establish that the dealer had the kind of furniture that JC was looking for. He did, so they hitched the trailer to the back of the Volvo and started optimistically on their way.

It was a cool evening, with a few clouds and the promise of a pleasant day to follow. Alice had decided to come along for the ride, so Jack sat in the back with the inevitable can of Coke. As they drove down the country lanes of the Welsh countryside

Brian's mind was full of the job that they were engaged upon. JC was quite forgotten as he steered the Volvo deftly round the narrow country lanes.

Shipping furniture to the States a few years ago was a lot easier than it is now. Furniture was more plentiful then, and articles that are now put into containers and sent abroad, would not have been sent a few years ago. Strictly speaking an antique has to be a hundred years old, but because America is such a young country anything pre war was hungrily snapped up. Brian had lost count of the number of draw-leaf tables, chairs, 1930 china cabinets, wardrobes, hallstands and washstands that he had sent to the States, and of course the inevitable piano was always wanted.

It is a sad fact of life that it is only now, when most of this type of furniture has been shipped abroad that we realise what we have lost by sending our heritage across the Atlantic.

Unfortunately furniture now is made of chipboard and chrome, and only made to last a few years. It is what the youth of today wants, it is what society has proclaimed is the fashion. The furniture that is made of solid wood (thank goodness there are still some manufacturers who do make it) will be the antiques of tomorrow.

As they drove through the moonlit night in search of JC's stock, the Bantam was quite unaware of the scarcity that would come in a few years time, and the price that one would have to pay for furniture in the future.

Jack had set a budget of three thousand pounds for his container, in another eight or nine years that would increase to ten or twelve thousand pounds for the same amount of furniture.

'What was that,' Alice cried, suddenly pulling herself upright in the seat, turning to face Jack who was sitting in the back sipping his Coke and full of his own thoughts.

'You what Love?' Brian murmured, uninterestedly, his thoughts miles away.

'I thought I felt something, didn't you?' she said, looking at the Bantam with trepidation on her face.

'Hey Jack,' Brian said quietly, looking at him through the rear view mirror, 'how is the trailer?'

'Trailer, what trailer? I didn't know we had a trailer with us, because there sure is not one there now,' replied Jack in surprise, his can of Coke falling to the floor.

'Damn!' exclaimed Brian savagely, and angrily pulled the car to the side of the road. 'The bloody trailer has gone! How the hell did that happen? We had better get out and look for the damn thing.'

Eventually, after about half an hour, they found the trailer lying on its back in a water-filled ditch. When he attached it to the car, he must have omitted to connect the safety chain. A bump in the road must have jerked the ball hitch and sent the trailer across the road and into the ditch.

JC laughed like mad, as Brian, shamefaced and angry at himself at his omission, dragged the offending trailer out of the water and reconnected it, making sure this time that the safety chain was firmly attached. They eventually arrived at their destination a little later than anticipated, but at least no harm had been done, and Brian quietly vowed to himself that in future he would double check the hitch before he set out anywhere.

At the dealer's Brian left Jack to buy the furniture that he required. JC browsed through the stacks of old furniture that were piled up high on either side of the warehouse, and, from time to time he would call across to confer or to check a price. This was his show, the Bantam was only being paid to drive him around to dealers who had decent stock and who would not rip him off. That would not have been easy anyway because Jack was a shrewd man and nobody's fool.

Then Brian saw it. It was sitting on the floor in a corner, half hidden behind a large Victorian chest of drawers. On the top was a pile of prints and a large painting of a stag at bay almost hidden from view. If it had not been for a shaft of light striking the corner of polished oak, that protruded behind the picture, Brian might have missed it.

It was a magnificent eighteenth century mule chest. About four feet wide standing two feet six inches in height. It had a three panelled top and two drawers at the base. It was covered in a profusion of original carving and the drawers still had the original brass swan neck handles that had been put on over two hundred years ago.

'A donkey box,' the Bantam murmured to himself as he lovingly ran his fingers over the smooth, time worn surface.

'An original donkey box.' He smiled to himself as he used the slang term that was used in the trade to describe a mule chest, that had two drawers in the base. Unlike a blanket chest that had no drawers at all.

Quite often over the years the bottom of a mule chest would rot, due to the continual washing of the stone floors that they inevitably stood upon; it was a simple matter then to remove the drawers and cut it down so that it resembled a blanket chest. Brian was certain that there were many people who owned a blanket chest, who were in complete ignorance of the fact that it started life as a mule chest.

As he removed the pile of prints from the top and looked in admiration at the black oak carving, he thought of all the tales that it could tell of the many people who had owned it over the years, and their joy and heartaches over all the decades that had passed.

'Hey Bantam.' He was immediately brought back to reality by JC's booming voice and his heavy hand on his shoulder. 'come and see what you think of this.' And as he reluctantly turned way from the mule chest, he made a mental note to enquire about it after Jack had completed his business.

Whilst Brian had been inspecting the chest, JC had been buying quite a lot of furniture, and they would be hard pressed to get it all on the car roof rack and the small trailer. But Brian was determined to obtain the mule chest, so whilst JC supervised the loading of the Volvo, he struck a deal for the chest at a very reasonable price.

At long last they were ready to return home, and Brian

prudently checked the safety chain to make sure that there were no repeat performances of the lost trailer.

Alice had been over the moon with the chest. 'I know exactly where I am going to put it,' she gushed, as Brian carefully secured it to the top of the load.

'You might just have to put it into the shop,' he laughed, making reference to the fact that they were planning to open an antique shop, instead of doing all the business from home as they were doing at present.

'Oh no love,' Alice cried, clutching at his arm, a look of horror on her face, 'it's far too nice to sell. Can't we keep it? Please.'

Brian laughed at the expression and patted her arm, 'Certainly you can keep it my love, I was only joking.'

'Will it be safe?' she asked nervously, as he fingered the rope securing the furniture to the trailer.

'Of course it will,' he replied, grinning at the doubtful expression on her face. 'I've had a lot more furniture on than this lot. Jump in and let's get going. 'His answer was true. He used to think nothing of loading furniture onto the Volvo and stacking it three tiers high. He had often thought of sending a photograph to Volvo to get their reaction to the misuse of their vehicle, but he never did get around to it.

'Hey Jack,' he called, as he climbed behind the wheel. 'What do you say to a pint of genuine English beer on the way home?' But JC had had enough for one night and had dropped off to sleep, his head resting on the top of a rather nice Victorian porter's chair that protruded over the back of the seat.

'Jammy bugger,' the Bantam thought to himself as he wended his way through the late night traffic. 'Here I am going round the country every day for years and I have never seen a porter's chair. JC comes over from America and in a couple of days one drops into his lap, just like that. Some people have all the luck.

After the night's work Brian fancied a drink, and although JC said that he was tired, Brian did finally manage to persuade him to have one on the way home. They called in at a quiet little country pub about twenty miles from home, for about half an hour, and for the remainder of the journey JC raved on and on about how wonderful the English pubs were, or ale houses, as he insolently called them. It was close to twelve thirty by the time they arrived home, and Brian was feeling dead beat. But he unloaded into the warehouse, and the precious donkey box had to be taken into the house. As he started to untie the ropes on the roof rack, Alice let out a piercing scream which nearly made Brian's heart stop with fright.

'What the hell is wrong?' he said, whirling to face her, a scared look on his face.

Alice pointed to the trailer with a shaking finger, 'The box has gone,' she said. 'It's bloody well gone!'

The Bantam followed her gaze and saw for himself that she was indeed right. His lovely chest was no longer where he had tied it. The rope had broken and it must have fallen off somewhere along the road.

'I remember seeing it when we left the pub,' Alice murmured thoughtfully, 'and it was still tied on then.'

They had no alternative but to retrace their tracks and hope that nobody had picked it up or run over it.

'This really is not my night,' Brian cursed to himself, as he retraced his tracks and, after driving about fifteen miles he was beginning to despair of ever seeing the chest again. It would be a long time before he would find such a perfect mule chest and he was quite upset that they might have lost it for good. He cursed again as he sped through the quiet countryside, his eyes anxiously scanning the road.

'Cheer up old son.' JC patted his shoulder affectionately. 'We'll find it all right, just you see.' And true enough, as they rounded the next corner the headlights shone on an unbelievable sight. Sitting squarely in the middle of the road, for all the world like a dog waiting for its master, was the mule chest. Cars must have been forced to drive around it as it was slap bang in the middle of the road, and as if to prove a point at that moment a car sped quickly round the bend, swerving to avoid it, the driver mouthing unheard curses at the obstruction.

'Christ,' murmured Brian, 'somebody could have bloody well been killed. Come on Jack, give me a hand,' and they quickly scrambled out of the car to retrieve the wayward chest.

'The rope must have snapped as we rounded the bend and it just slid off into the middle of the road,' Alice said soberly, as they quickly retrieved it and tied it securely to the top of the Volvo. 'Thank God we found it all right.'

'Thank God there wasn't an accident,' echoed JC, and it was in a sober mood that they slowly drove home.

Brian still has the oak mule chest to this day. Dealers have come and gone, but the donkey box still sits quietly in its position at the top of the stairs waiting for its next owner to come along, and whenever Brian passes it he gives a little smile to himself as he remembers the day that he nearly lost it.

Chapter Four

JC's Box

A few weeks later found Brian and Alice installed in their new premises.

It was a medium sized shop with a large five roomed flat above and very large yard at the rear which would enable them to build a large storage facility and a workshop, with enough space in which to put a forty foot container. There was also a large area that could be roofed over in which to put a stripping patch, as Brian was going to strip his own furniture, much to JC's delight.

They also acquired Alf.

Alf it must be said, was an enigma, the powers that be must have broken the mould after they produced him. About fifty years old, he stood over six feet tall, and was as broad as a barn door. His fists were like legs of ham, and he had a face that reminded one of an old bloodhound. Unfortunately, due to an accident in his childhood he was a little slow on the uptake. But for all that, Alf had a heart of gold, would do anything for anybody, and was passionately fond of children. This got him into trouble on more than one occasion when he had tried to give them sweets, or a coin, without having any ulterior motive in his head at all, but unfortunately people have suspicious minds, and he received a lot of undeserved abuse.

Brian had taken Alf under his wing, and Alf for his part, stripped all the pine furniture and doors that came into the shop, and was very grateful for the extra money, as he hadn't held down a regular job for years.

He was also immensely strong and came in very handy when it came to moving furniture and packing containers. Unfortunately he was completely devoid of humour. You could say anything to Alf, however derogatory, and it would go completely over his head.

It was about this time that JC's box arrived.

It sat on its ten wheel bogie in the middle of the yard, like a replica of the Mersey Tunnel. Its cavernous interior seemingly to go on and on forever, and its huge entrance like a giant gaping mouth.

It was JC's first container. Forty feet in length, eight feet high and seven feet six inches wide. It was massive, and the thought of having to fill it tightly with JC's furniture made the Bantam feel a little nervous. It was the first time he had ever filled a forty foot box. He had filled twenty foot boxes, but forty was a different matter. As he made his way across the yard, avoiding the puddles left by the previous night's rain, he doubted that he had enough furniture to fill it. He was also hoping the weather would change before he started packing it, as there is nothing worse than trying to pack in the pouring rain. The corrugated paper gets wet, and the furniture gets wet as it is being carried from the warehouse to the container. The forecast said that it would be fine, so Brian was keeping his fingers tightly crossed.

He made his way into the warehouse to where JC's furniture was stacked high along one wall. On every item a large white sticky label gave the manifest number and any information relevant to the piece. These stickers were very important, because on arrival in America, customs officials checked each item against the manifest. Any discrepancy would mean a heavy fine for the owner, and he had actually heard of a dealer who had to fly out to the States to sort out a problem with a fault on a manifest.

Each sticker must also show how many pieces the item contains, for example a draw-leaf table has four, the base, two leaves, and the top, and each piece must have a sticker on it because during the packing they may be in separate parts of the box. The paperwork for the shipment of a container must be accurate to prevent a hold up at the docks, which could be for days.

Brian walked slowly to the rear of the warehouse to check that he had enough rolls of card and tape to start the packing the next day. There is a surprising amount of work in packing a container, as each item has to be individually wrapped in the corrugated card and sealed with tape, making certain the smooth side of the paper is against the smooth surface of the wood, to avoid marking the polished surface. The Bantam well remembered seeing a container of furniture that had been wrapped the wrong way. All the polished surfaces had long marks running down them. These were impossible to remove and every piece had to be re-polished.

Strange things happen to furniture as it travels the seaways of the world. The Bantam recalled once sending a container to Los Angeles, that arrived with every piece of furniture covered in green mould. He had rented a large old chicken shed, to use as a warehouse, from a local farmer who had used it to breed chickens. The shed had a dirt floor that had packed down over the years. Brian had unsuspectingly stored the furniture on top of this and the damp had permeated into every piece of furniture. Consequently when the ship sailed into the warmer climate of America the temperature in the box rose and the horrible green fungus grew over everything. Needless to say the recipient was absolutely furious and Brian lost a very good customer, as well as a lot of money, as the customer refused to pay the agreed amount. The Bantam had been very glad it was a twenty foot box and not a forty foot one, as they hold more than double the amount of goods.

As he turned to leave the warehouse and extinguish the lights, his mind still full of the memories of what he now laughingly called the Fungus Box, his gaze fell on a beautiful rosewood Victorian upright over-strung piano. This was JC's pride and joy, he had paid well for it and wished that he could have bought a dozen at the same price. It was a beautiful thing, Brian slowly and lovingly ran his fingers over the silky wood and admired the grain in the veneer, and the octagonal tapered legs which supported it.

As he did so his thoughts again went back to the first container that he ever sent to America and the first piece of furniture that went into it. A grand piano. After removing the legs, the Bantam had placed the piano on its side up against the end of the container. In front of it he had put an old spring interior mattress which had come out of a house full of furniture that he had recently cleared. Up against that, to hold it all firmly in place, he had put a large, heavy, oak, mirror fronted wardrobe. Unfortunately he did not realise that with the continuous stopping and starting of the container lorry, the piano was being constantly banged against the side of the box by the springs of the mattress, consequently by the time it reached its destination, it was very badly damaged and in a very sorry state indeed.

It had served to teach Brian yet one more lesson. It made him realise that most of the damage is done to the furniture when it is being driven to and from the docks. Not when it is on the water.

'Don't worry Jack, my old son,' he said to himself softly, as he carefully locked the door to the warehouse, 'I will make certain that your pride and joy reaches you intact and in good condition,' and he gave a little grin to himself. After that experience he always made certain to pack pianos very, very carefully.

To make a container a financially viable proposition, the secret is to pack as much furniture in as possible. China cabinets are put inside wardrobes, chairs are interwoven into the bases of tables, which are, in turn, stacked on top of teach other. Drawers are filled with bric-a-brac tightly packed to prevent movement. Every available space is filled to capacity. A cat would have a hard time finding a home in a properly packed container.

JC had returned to America a few days earlier, being quite content to leave the packing and exporting of his box to Brian. Before he had left, he had shaken the Bantam's hand in a grip that threatened to break his fingers, and had left it to Brian to buy any more furniture that would be needed to fill the container. Brian knew the type of furniture that JC wanted, so with a puff of grey smoke from his King Edward cigar, JC had jumped into his taxi and was gone.

For his part, Brian was obviously going to pack the box as tight as he could. If he could get all JC's furniture in and still leave room, then he would be able to buy more and send him the bill for the extra.

Next day, true to the weatherman's forecast, dawned bright and clear. The sun was drying the wet ground from the previous day's rain with the hope of a warm day to come. The lads that he had hired to help him pack the container, plus Alf, who was as eager to start as a dog straining at the leash, on hearing the word 'walkies', were each carrying a piece of furniture across the yard, checking that each item had a sticker on it. For their part Alice and Brian were securely wrapping each piece of furniture and putting it in its place in the box.

'It's like doing a jigsaw puzzle,' laughed Alice, as she carefully stacked a chair on top of a wardrobe. They all worked very hard and by lunchtime were about ten feet into the container. It had all gone nicely so far without any awkward bits of furniture to slow them down. An odd shaped piece can really cause a problem until it is secured, but so far everything was as sweet as a nut. Alf had worked as hard as two men and still looked completely tireless and eager to continue, and Brian thought himself very lucky that he had found him, in spite of his drawbacks.

By lunchtime the following day, they were about twenty feet into the box and it was beginning to look to Brian as if he was going to be short of furniture. He looked at the manifest for the umpteenth time, because he was trying to gauge what was left, and if he needed to go out and buy more. They continued to pack and about five feet from the end they ran out of furniture.

Secretly Brian was quite pleased, the container was tightly packed and there was still room for him to put more in. Alf complained in a loud voice, 'We ain't got no more gear to put in Guv, there's a load of old empty crates in the lock up, shall we put them in to fill the empty space?'

Brian smiled at the thought of JC's face if he did as Alf had suggested and filled the remaining five feet with empty packing cases. He would have had a fit, and he had to spend the next few minutes explaining to Alf why the container must be full of furniture.

'But we haven't got any, have we Guv?' bemoaned Alf, 'What are we gonna do?'

'Don't worry about it Alf,' replied Brian as he laughingly patted Alf's arm, 'we'll get some more furniture to put in it.'

Alice for her part, was concerned that Jack wouldn't send a cheque for the extra furniture.

'Don't worry, Pet, Brian smiled affectionately, he'll send it, if he doesn't I will do a Paul Daniels on him,' and they both burst out laughing.

The reason for their laughter, was the memory of an incident that happened to a fellow dealer that they knew, who also shipped to the States. He had a customer who had bought a couple of containers from him with no trouble at all. The client had paid him and requested that he send another box to him with as much bric-a-brac as he could fit in, this of course increased the value of the shipment. The dealer was not unduly worried, his client had paid in the past. So he, unsuspectingly sent the container and sat back to await payment. After about three months and many demands, he still had not received anything. Then a letter arrived saying that his client had been ill in hospital, was now recovered, and would Paul please send another box and he would be paid for this one in a couple of weeks time.

Paul agreed, and sent the required shipment, duly receiving, by return of post, a bank draft from America for the previous box. He laughed when he recounted the story to the Bantam over a drink, during a break from a sale that they were at a few weeks later.

'I would love to have seen his face when he opened the box and found it completely empty,' he chuckled. It was worth the shipping cost to get my money back!' and he chortled at the picture of his client opening a container with not a stick of furniture inside.

Brian spent the next couple of days going around the trade to find the extra furniture that was needed to finish JC's box off. Time was running out, a dock strike was being hinted at, and the shipping company wanted their container ship to sail as soon as possible, consequently they wanted to collect the container the next day. They all worked through the day and into the night to meet the deadline. They were getting to the end which is very important, because it if was not packed tightly enough the contents would have a chance to move, and possibly break.

Thinking about the extra furniture he would need, Brian opened the drawer of an Edwardian wardrobe that he had bought from a dealer that day. He had told the Bantam that it had just come from a house clearance. Brian had a mirror in his hands ready to put it in, when something caught his eye. As he pulled the drawer it jerked open, and there sitting in the middle of the drawer was a rolled up bundle of five pound notes! Brian was astounded, he had no idea where the wardrobe had come from the dealer he had bought it from was not one of his regulars, it had been bought from a secondhand shop that he had happened to pass. So with a large smile on his face he put the roll of notes in his pocket. By now it was getting late and they still had the next morning to finish off the container so they called it a day, and on the strength of his find, Brian took everybody to the local pub to celebrate his windfall.

Feeling very content, and mellow after a good meal and a few drinks, Alice and Brian arrived home about midnight. As they came through the door, Brian could hear the shrill insistent ringing of the telephone. He really didn't want to answer it, he just wanted to go to bed, but he thought that it might be important. It was. It was the shipping company, they had been trying to reach him all evening. They were coming in the morning to pick up the container, the dock strike was on!

Alice and the Bantam always remembered finishing off Jack Cummin's container. Dressed in their best finery, suffering from an over indulgence of drink, and with the compliments of a changed weather forecast, soaked to the skin, they eventually, in the early hours of the morning finally closed the large clamps on the doors of the container.

But they did beat the dock strike.

And JC received his box on time.

Chapter Five

The Copper Kettle

The silence hit the Bantam like a physical blow, as he slowly and carefully walked down the steep steps that led into the witness box. On his left, almost within touching distance, sat the judge, traditionally dressed in his purple and red robes, a curled wig on his head, looking very stern and imposing, as he viewed the courtroom in front of him.

He must be about seventy years of age, Brian thought to himself as he entered the box. With his sombre face and watery eyes, that gazed into Brian's, as they faced each other across the courtroom, he made the Bantam quite nervous.

He was sitting in a high backed carved oak chair that had VR expertly cut into its back, on the wall above and behind him, hung the royal coat of arms. It all looked very impressive and made Brian feel very small and insignificant.

His hands began to perspire and his legs started to tremble, as he began to realise what is meant when people talk about 'the full majesty of the law'.

Opposite him sat the jury, sitting in three rows of four people to each row, making up the mandatory 'twelve men good and true', but in this case, there were seven men and five women.

His first reaction was how young they all looked, or was he getting old? Good God, he was only twenty nine years old himself when all was said and done, but to Brian's mind not one of them looked old enough to sit in judgement on his fellow men.

His eyes fell upon the bewigged and gowned barristers who sat on the long benches beneath him scanning through their briefs, seemingly not to be concerned as to what was going on around them.

He was to find out later that they would be like a cat playing with a mouse, and when they were ready to pounce would show no mercy.

Behind and above the barristers stood the dock containing the prisoner and his police escort. The policeman standing stiffly, stern faced, slightly behind the prisoner, whose eyes were never still.

As the Bantam gazed across at the dock, all he could see was a mop of black curly air and a pair of cold green eyes that stared into his. The prisoner was leaning insolently against the side of the dock, and from the Bantam's position he gave the impression of being very small, but the Bantam knew different. The prisoner was at least six feet in height as well he remembered.

Brian gazed up at the vast domed ceiling of the courtroom as the sunlight streamed through the stained glass windows giving the impression that he was in church, instead of the Crown Court of her most Britannic Majesty.

He pondered about the architectural design of the circular courtroom with its old oak panelling and its fine oak carvings.

The walls were hung with oil paintings of past sheriffs of the city, all with sombre faces and eyes that seemed to follow you whichever way you turned.

A fine example of an eighteenth century Parliament clock hung on the wall, gazing silently down on the proceedings; and much to Brian's surprise hanging incongruously beneath it, was a modern black plastic electric clock, that looked completely out of place and quite revolting. He wondered why it had been put there, and later that day he found out that it had been placed there because the court did not employ a janitor, so consequently there was nobody to wind the three antique clocks that hung in the various courtrooms (all with electric clocks hanging beneath them).

Volunteers to wind the clocks had been refused permission in case they fell off the ladder, presumably because of insurance purposes, the electric clocks had been put up instead! The Bantam thought it very strange, rather sad, and very perplexing.

As he studied the scene that lay before him, his glance fell again on the bewigged and gowned barristers that were still busy going through their paperwork, and reflected that when Queen Mary had died back in 1694 the barristers of the country had donned long black gowns as a sign of morning and respect. And they were still wearing them to this very day, nearly three hundred years later.

This is the fabric of British tradition, he thought, as his eyes scanned the room, the fabric that so many countries throughout the world have tried to emulate. His hands shook slightly as he stood nervously anticipating the ordeal that was to come.

His thoughts went back to John Adams, who could quite easily have been standing in the dock instead of the hapless prisoner. In fact, Brian thought to himself, he is probably more guilty of stealing than the man in the dock.

It had been about six months previously that Brian had been having a quiet drink with John Adams, a dealer friend of his. They were sitting at the bar of the Golden Lion, a lovely old Welsh country inn that nestled between the green hills of North Wales. It was the sort of pub that you would only find if you took the trouble to drive around the narrow twisting winding lanes that littered the countryside, but once you had found it, you would always return.

The old eighteenth century pine settle still sat snugly in the same corner that it had sat for decades. The walls were adorned with family photographs of the landlord's ancestors and antique artefacts were in abundance. The landlord and his wife were a lovely caring couple who still had the idea (which is unfortunately seldom found today) that they needed the customer, and not the other way around. In fact when time was called, Paul the landlord would be found standing by the door bidding goodnight to his customers, much as the local vicar would bid farewell to his parishioners on Sunday mornings.

On Saturday nights the place would come alive as all the local farmers and their families would gather around the organ, and the beautiful sound of Welsh voices raised in song would echo around the hills.

The Bantam's favourite character at the Golden Lion was an old man called Cy Bach. He was a small man with a lovable weatherbeaten face that reminded him somewhat of a garden gnome with his ruddy complexion, white hair and his piercing blue eyes that seemed to look right through you.

He was a typical Welsh farmer who lived on a forty acre farm up in the hills, he was about sixty years of age, a fascinating sense of humour, and a permanent smile upon his worldly face.

He interested Brian, as with a glass of whiskey and lemonade in his hand, and a faraway look in his eyes, he would tell of the ways of the Welsh farmer, both past and present. Of how he trained his sheepdogs to obey, not as one would expect with a whistled command, but one that was given in sign language with the occasional verbal command. He explained to him the process of silage (the winter food processed for the cattle), how important it was that the silage pits were properly sealed, and how the silage was usually ready for eating in about four weeks from the laying down in the pit.

But when Cy opened his mouth to sing it was as if the archangels themselves were singing. To Brian's ears, it was out of this world.

Cy's recitations had him spellbound. Every voice in the Golden Lion would be still and you could hear a pin drop as he recited in his lilting Welsh voice the saga of 'The Old Man'.

Even though he couldn't speak a word of this beautiful language (his father had spoken it fluently but hadn't thought it important to teach his son), Brian would still feel tingles running down his spine as he listened to Cy Bach. He would marvel at the talent that could put so much feeling into, what was to him, a completely alien language. And yet, the same man who had such tender emotional feelings could quite happily raise a flock of sheep to send for slaughter without compunction. But each to his own. After all, Brian thought, Cy Bach probably couldn't go into a house where the owner had recently died and sift through his lifelong possessions without any feeling of emotion, as he had trained himself to do.

John Adams however was a strange character, having a Jewish mother and a Welsh father, but having very strong leanings to Judaism and the Jewish way of life. On the surface he was a likeable chap who you would be quite happy to buy a second hand car from, but underneath lay a hard ruthless streak that Brian would find quite impossible to emulate, as over the years he had tried to do, because deep down he was a softy. 'A sucker for anybody with a hard luck story' as Alice was always quick to point out.

As they sat quietly at their table drinking, Brian was unaware of the surprises that the evening had in store for him as John was yet again trying to teach him about the ways of the world. John was about forty years of age, about five feet nine inches tall, with dark wavy hair that was going grey at the temples. He had deep brown eyes that seemed to look into your very soul as he looked at you, and a long roman nose that betrayed his fondness for whiskey.

He was the Bantam's mentor and he trusted him implicitly. John taught him all about the antiques trade and about people, most of all he taught him about life, and how to survive in this uncaring world of ours.

He taught him how to handle the problems of life by putting each one in a little mental box of its own, and only opening the box when you were ready to face it. A feat that took the Bantam a long, long time to accomplish, but when he had, he found that he could face life's problems with no trouble. But John did nothing for nothing, and it was to be a few years later that Brian realised that for years John had been using him, and that in many ways, he had made John a lot of money.

But John's teachings had done him a lot of good because he was now beginning to understand what people and life were all about.

John did not approve of Alice, he thought that Brian could do better, but Brian, true to form did not listen to a word that John had said. Time was to prove that John was right. The time was to come when he would admit that John had been right about a great many things.

True enough, he was learning, life with Alice was good, he was building up the business and he was making money. But the black clouds were approaching slowly across the horizon.

'What's up,' Brian enquired casually, as he took yet another sip of his fast diminishing drink, 'there's twenty minutes to go yet before they throw us out.'

'We must go very soon,' John replied quickly, looking at his watch yet again, 'I have to get back to the farm, I have an appointment to keep.'

'An appointment,' surprise registered on Brian's face, 'at this time of night? Who the hell are you going to meet at this ungodly hour?'

'You will see Bantam,' John grinned, 'you will see. Come on, drink up, we must be off,' and he quickly threw back the remnants of his glass of whiskey and slowly pushed his way through the crowded bar towards the door. Mystified, Brian obediently followed him out into the night, pulling up his collar against the cold wind that heralded a frosty night to come.

John was very quiet on the way back to the farm, actually it was an old seventeenth century building with about an acre of land and a lot of outbuildings that he had bought for a song a few years back because it was slowly falling into ruins. After a lot of hard work (and money) he had finally restored it to its original condition and it now stood in splendour, a tribute to the dedication of its new owner.

'Listen,' he growled sternly at Brian as he slid quickly behind the wheel of the inevitable Volvo estate car, 'what you are about to see tonight you must never divulge to a living soul, if I find out that you have told anyone, I'll flay you alive. Got it!'

'Of course I won't,' Brian retorted in a hurt tone, 'you know me better than that, I wouldn't tell anyone your business.'

And it was true, he would never have told anyone John's secrets, he had his complete and utter loyalty.

As they drove slowly into John's spacious yard, surrounded by all the outbuildings, he could see a black Luton van parked discretely under the trees, its lights off and almost invisible in the darkness of the night.

There was a glow of a cigarette from the driver's side as the doors opened and two scruffily dressed young men jumped out on their arrival. They shook John's hand warmly and commenced to talk to each other in low tones, occasionally glancing across at the Bantam, who was quite bemused by what was going on.

The younger of the two men was dressed in denim jeans and a scruffy blue sweatshirt, whilst the elder of the two was wearing a dark blue suit over a white open necked shirt and brown shoes. Both were unshaven and to Brian's eyes looked decidedly unsavoury and very tired, which as he found out later was hardly surprising, as they had just driven non-stop through the night from Edinburgh.

Brian gave a start of surprise as they started to unload the van, John gave him a warning look and shook his head slightly from side to side, putting his finger to his lips as he did so. It took the men a good half an hour to unload the black van, which turned out to contain a veritable treasure trove of antiques. Old paintings, wall clocks, silver, bronze, furniture, the list was endless, and all were in pristine condition. As each piece was taken into the storeroom, John and the elder of the two men would barter until a satisfactory price for each piece had been met, and it had been carefully stored away. In about an hour, all the arrangements had been made and John quickly disappeared into the farm, to reappear a little while later carrying the largest pile of bank notes that the Bantam had ever seen.

'Eighteen and a half grand, right?' grinned John, and with an elaborate gesture counted the money into the older man's extended grubby hand. 'Give me a bell when you get some more,' he said cheerfully as they all walked over to the van talking in low tones and completely ignoring Brian, who by this time was quite bemused by the whole affair. Then John returned and with a little chuckle to himself, extinguished the lights, locked the door, and, which to Brian seemed quite ironic, switched on the burglar alarm.

The silence was overwhelming and endless as the barrister stood up and shuffled the pile of papers that lay before him with unconcerned confidence, and the stenographer looked up in anticipation.

The clerk of the court passed the Bantam a bible and bid him repeat the words on the card that lay on the ledge before him. As he repeated the oath, his voice reverberated around the room carried by the sensitive microphone that stood in front of him, and once again he trembled.

He looked across at the dock and once again rued the day that he met the prisoner, and it was all because of a copper kettle, he thought angrily to himself, as he removed his hand from the bible.

It had been about three months previously on a cold, wet, windy Monday morning, and Brian was once again suffering from an overindulgence of Canadian Club from the night before, a practice that had become more frequent of late.

'Hey mate,' the young man had called insolently as he roughly pushed open the door of the shop and strolled arrogantly in, 'Do you buy stuff?' The Bantam looked slowly up from the newspaper that he had been reading and took an instant dislike to the dark haired youth that stood before him. He was dressed in the regulation pair of faded blue jeans, a grubby green tee-shirt, with a pair of dirty black trainers on his feet. Around his neck was a tattooed rope with the words 'Cut here' emblazoned below. He carried a supermarket bag in his hand.

'Yes,' Brian replied coldly, as he stood carefully up from his chair and put the newspaper down on his desk. He did not appreciate the interruption, as his head was pounding.

'Yes, I do. What have you got?'

The youth put his hand into the carrier bag and extracted the most beautiful large brass and copper kettle that he had ever seen in his life. It was a magnificent example of Victorian metalwork, with a brass and copper handle, and the telltale castle joints down the back and around the base.

'Where did you get it?' Brian enquired, as he ran his hands over the smooth, gleaming surface.

'Me Mam died a couple of months ago,' the young man replied, plonking himself unceremoniously down into a beautiful Victorian nursing chair, with complete disregard for his greasy trousers on its delicate pink covering.

The Bantam's dislike for him increased.

'Give us seventy quid,' the youth said, drawing greedily on his cigarette and blowing the smoke towards Brian.

It made Brian cough and regret yet again his excesses of the previous evening. In retrospect, he should have known better than to buy the copper kettle from the young lad, but he wasn't feeling himself and he couldn't wait to get the uncouth chap out of his shop.

Eventually after a lot of haggling they finally settled on a price of fifty pounds, which satisfied Brian, as he knew that he could get a reasonable profit on it.

The youth finally sauntered out of the shop, stuffing the cash into his pocket and scattering cigarette ash all around him as he left.

Brian, for his part, was glad to be rid of him. He did not know exactly what made him do it, perhaps it was a sixth sense, perhaps the powers that be were taking care of him again, but before the lad left, Brian asked to see some identification, and he wrote it down in his call book.

It was that simple action that saved him from standing in the dock instead of the witness box, on a charge of receiving stolen goods.

As it eventually transpired, the young lad had stolen the copper kettle from his sister. It had been left to his sister in their mother's will after she had died from a heart attack two months previously. He was a drug addict and was short of money to feed his habit and had stolen it from his sister, having scant regard for their relationship. The fact that he had given the Bantam his correct address only went to prove how stupid he was.

Eventually after a long and exhausting cross examination, in which the prosecuting counsel did his best to incriminate him, Brian was allowed to leave the witness box and he made his way into the waiting room and welcoming cup of tea.

As he slowly sipped his tea, he thought how traumatic it must be to stand in the dock as the accused.

He thought about the democratic system of this country, the cost of the barristers, the jury, and all the paperwork that was involved in a court case.

We take for granted the democratic system that we have in this country and the fact that a person is innocent until proven guilty.

Needless to say, Brian lost his fifty pounds, but he was determined to be more careful in the future. It was another lesson that he had learnt in the great school of life, and one that he would never forget.

He remembered the words that John had said to him a few weeks previously.

'Always remember, Bantam, whatever happens to you in this short life, be it a good experience, or a bad one, remember it and learn from it and it would not have happened in vain.'

And for the rest of his life, the Bantam did just that.

Chapter Six

The Corner Cupboard

The Bantam had forgotten exactly how he became interested in the mysterious world of pine stripping.

In retrospect, it was probably John Adams who had introduced him to it, and to Sodium Hydroxide, which was the correct name for Caustic Soda, the agent that was used to remove the paint from furniture and doors.

Until recent years antique pine was generally regarded by most people as a lower class of furniture, antique dealers would deride it and regard it as an inferior type of furniture.

'Oh it's only pine,' they used to say with scorn, when faced with a piece of furniture. Unlike today when the expression is quite the opposite.

Today pine is becoming very popular and is being widely reproduced because of the scarcity of the antique originals. People are starting to appreciate the fine golden colour of pine and the country look. Preferring it to the chrome and plastic of recent years.

A pine dresser that could have been purchased fifteen years ago for twenty five pounds, today would cost nearer two hundred and fifty pounds, and will continue to rise in value at the same rate as other antiques are doing.

It was only recently that Brian had seen a large circular pine

Loo table sitting in the window of a local antique shop masquerading as a mid nineteenth century pine table.

On closer inspection it turned out to be a pine table certainly, but at one time it had been veneered, and had probably started life as a mid nineteenth century mahogany loos table veneered on a pine carcase, but over the years the veneer had disappeared and it was now just a memory of its former glory.

Today's modern methods have made the stripping of pine furniture a great deal easier than it used to be, and a lot less hazardous.

Pine stripping was, and in many cases still is, done by dealers who would be equipped with a large metal tank, about eight feet log, four feet wide and three feet high, filled with Sodium Hydroxide. This would be large enough to completely immerse a piece of furniture and would sometimes be heated by a gas heater positioned underneath the tank.

The biggest drawback with a heated tank is that although it does the job quicker, it gives off a lot of dangerous fumes. It was because of this that the Bantam decided to have an unheated tank.

Brian well remembered an occasion when Alf had a crystal of Caustic Soda in his eye. He had been refilling the stripping tank with water and putting extra Caustic Soda in it to bring it up to strength. Instead of gently slitting the plastic bag of Caustic, Alf had attacked it with a knife, in the manner of a homicidal maniac attacking his victim. Consequently, the crystals of Caustic were scattered about everywhere and one found its way into Alf's eye. Fortunately for Alf he had one of his rare moments of common sense and turned the hosepipe of clear cool water straight into his face.

In spite of that, Alf was taken, reluctantly and complaining bitterly all the way, to the hospital because, as the Bantam was at pains to point out to Alf, he could easily have been blinded.

Alf, although not one of the world's brightest specimens, had enough brains to see an opportunity presenting itself. He turned to Brian on the way to the hospital and said, mournfully, 'I reckon

I should get more money for this job. It's bloody dangerous. I could have been blinded you know Guv. I reckon I deserve more money. Don't you?'

'No, I bloody well don't,' snapped back the Bantam, trying to hide a grin. 'If you had been a bit more careful, and worn the goggles that are there for you, it would never have happened.

Alf, realising that there was going to be no extra money to be made from the situation, sulked all the way to the hospital.

The secret of good pine stripping is to make certain that the piece of furniture is not left for too long in the tank. If it is, the joints become unglued, and there is a very real danger that the piece of furniture will finish up as pieces of wood floating aimlessly around on the surface of the tank.

Brian used to have a little chuckle to himself whenever he recalled the night that he took Alice out to a party after putting a pine chest of drawers in the stripping tank and forgetting about it.

On his return a few hours later, to his horror, he found the chest of drawers floating gently on the surface of the Caustic, about to separate into various separate pieces. With a yell of dismay, he quickly ran into the workshop, changed into his stripping gear, still being rather the worse for wear from the party, and managed to rescue it before too much damage was done.

The next morning, much to Alice's complete disgust, and to the Bantam's utter amazement, he woke up in bed still fully dressed in his dirty Caustic splashed stripping clothes, but minus his Wellingtons!

On inspection, his arms were found to be burned where the Caustic had splashed him, and one of his finger nails had turned black. This happened if there was a hole in the gloves allowing the Caustic to seep through.

'Serves you right,' Alice admonished him, as she gently bathed his burns. 'You should know better than to mess about at the tank in the state that you were in. You could have been badly hurt. Anyway,' she went on, 'it's high time you learnt that Caustic Soda deserves a little respect. You can't just treat it like water, you know.'

As Alice continued to remonstrate with him, Brian's mind wandered back to an incident that had once happened to him when he had been stripping a large pine dresser base.

He had been struggling to remove the heavy piece of furniture from the tank when it slipped through his fingers and fell back into the Caustic. The resulting splash, resembling a tidal wave, completely drenched him from the waist down in the lethal fluid.

The pain was excruciating, and with a loud scream of agony, he quickly ripped his trousers and underpants off and turned the hosepipe on to his private parts, which by this time, were suffering very painfully. As he lived in the upstairs flat, he dashed unthinkingly through the shop and up the stairs to the bedroom.

Unfortunately for Brian, there was an old lady in the shop at the time carefully examining a large, and expensive, cranberry vase, which she dropped with a scream of horror as he streaked past her, half naked, heading for the relief of the bathroom shower. It had been an extremely painful experience, but it always managed to bring a smile to his face when he recalled the look of horror on the old lady's face!

It was the practice of antique dealers to travel on regular routes, at regular times, calling on other dealers to buy stock. Few people realise that the piece of furniture they have just purchased from an antique shop has probably passed through half a dozen or more dealers' hands before ending up for sale to the public.

Travelling on a regular basis, dealers would get to know the type of furniture that was usually purchased and would make certain that they had the right items when the dealer called. They would also leave a profit in it, thus ensuring that they had a successful buying run and came back again.

Brian had a regular dealer who always called on a Thursday afternoon looking for mahogany Victorian furniture, so if Brian saw any on his buying trips he would buy them with this dealer in mind. He also had a dealer who came all the way from Belgium once a month, buying longcase clocks and period oak furniture. Another dealer would come on Fridays and be looking out for pine furniture. It was an arrangement that worked well for all the parties concerned, and they all made a profit.

Alice and Brian had been together now for about three years and Alice had decided that she would like to have a child. The prospect of fatherhood secretly terrified the Bantam. He didn't feel that he would be able to handle the responsibility of bringing up a child. He said nothing about his fears when Alice brought up the subject, just saying with a laugh and a large beaming grin on his face, 'Oh there's plenty of time yet for children, let's build up the business first and then think of starting a family,' and he would quickly change the subject.

But once again fate had decreed the Bantam's future because a few months later Alice happily announced to the world that she was to become a mother.

'I hope it's a girl darling.' Alice smiled contentedly over the dinner table. 'Don't you?' And she squeezed his hand.

'Let's put if this way love,' the Bantam replied cheerfully, 'if it's a girl, I'm going to send it back. If we are going to have anything, let's at least have a boy so that I can teach him the business.' And truth to tell, now that Brian had got used to the idea of becoming a father, he had developed a longing to have a son.

It was on a clear, frosty, November morning at five o'clock that the long awaited addition to the family arrived. She weighed seven pounds four ounces, had a shock of blonde hair and an exceptionally healthy pair of lungs.

Alice and Brian were delighted and decided to call her Ann, after Alice's mother.

One wet and windy Monday morning, a few weeks later, the Bantam decided that it was time he took a two day buying trip into the heart of Wales to see if he could find some pine. It was a bitterly cold morning and the dark sky was full of rolling black clouds, bringing the threat of a miserable day ahead. The sheep were huddled unhappily together against the dry stone walls that cut across the green landscape. They knew what the day was going to bring and that the dry stone wall would give some protection from the biting wind. Black and white Friesian cattle looked up as the Bantam drove slowly past, and then returned uninterested to their grazing.

'You wouldn't eat so much if you knew where you were going to finish up,' Brian chuckled out loud as he was forced to pull up quickly to avoid a tractor and trailer full of foul smelling manure negotiating the tricky entrance to a field ahead.

He was in a happy, relaxed frame of mind as he made his way from dealer to dealer. He was a father, and his heart was full of pride as he thought of his newly born daughter. He had had a good profitable day and was at peace with the world.

Many antique dealers worked from home, rather than have a shop, and as he drove along he kept a sharp lookout for the telltale 'Antiques' sign that would be nailed to a tree or a gatepost, to signify a home based dealer.

Brian preferred to deal with home based dealers, as he usually found that he could get on with them far better than a shopkeeper, whose usual cry on learning that he was in the trade would be 'Ten percent off for trade'. It was a trait that the Bantam hated as he liked to be able to wheel and deal when he was negotiating a price for a piece of furniture.

By mid afternoon the heavens had opened and the rain was coming down in sheets making driving very hazardous on the narrow twisting country lanes. So far he had had quite a good day's buying. Tied securely to the roof of the Volvo were a couple of rather nice pine kitchen tables, a set of six ladder backed chairs, a pine dresser base and a superb small pine Welsh dresser. It had a pretty shaped rack and a small dog kennel beneath (so called because the farmhouse dog would often sleep in it). It was a typical North Wales dresser which when stripped and waxed should realise a healthy profit.

As it happened, Brian eventually sold the dresser to a private customer for eighty pounds. The lady in question paid for it, then asked him to keep it in storage for her until the new house that was being built for her was ready. He kept it for two years, but the lady never returned to claim the property and the Bantam later resold it for a hundred pounds.

Fortunately, being made of pine, the furniture on the roof of the Volvo would not come to much harm from the rain, which was by now bouncing off the road with a tremendous force. After all, what harm could a little water do when the furniture was going to be drowned in a bath of Caustic Soda.

'Alf will be pleased with the load. It will give him something to do.' And he chuckled to himself.

The rain suddenly stopped, as if it had been turned off by an unseen hand, and the sun shone through a break in the clouds, like the beam of a torch in a blackened coal cellar.

Brian recalled the memory of Alf's face who, when returning a newly stripped door to a customer, learnt that the customer was going to repaint it. Alf was horrified, he had worked so hard to remove the paint and now the customer was going to cover his careful work with more layers of paint.

'How dare you paint it!' he stormed as the bemused gentleman struggled to put the now virgin clean door into the back of his estate car.

'I worked bloody hard stripping that door, and now you're going to paint it again! I don't know why you bloody well brought it here in the first place,' he raved on as the Bantam listened in amazement. But luckily the customer did not take offence, as, with a wink at Brian over Alf's shoulder, he faithfully promised not to repaint it.

Alf calmed down and with the parting shot, 'See that you don't, I worked hard on that,' he returned reluctantly to the stripping patch. Poor old Alf, Brian thought, smiling to himself, he really is a case, and he switched on his lights as dusk began to descend.

By six o'clock the Bantam had decided that enough was enough for one day. He was dog tired, and his eyes ached from the constant strain of peering through the driving rain. He would have to find a hotel, or a country pub to spend the night and get some rest, as he was dead beat. Half an hour later his prayers were answered when he found exactly what he wanted. It was a small country pub, sitting behind a pocket handkerchief of a car park, facing the rolling green hills, in a village whose Welsh name was quite unpronounceable.

Wearily pushing open the old, solid oak door that must have guarded the entrance for the last two hundred years, wiping the rain from his face as he did so, the Bantam entered the old pub. The warmth enveloped him like a favourite overcoat as he made his way slowly towards the dimly lit bar that lay directly in front of him.

His luck was holding. The pub only had two rooms to let, and both were vacant, and it was with a feeling of profound relief that he wearily signed the visitors book.

It was a typical old Welsh country pub with low, smoke stained ceilings, oak beams and an abundance of horse brasses and copper kettles hanging from every available space on the timber framed walls. A large log fire blazed cheerfully in the inglenook fireplace, the pleasant smell of burning wood permeating the bar, giving a feeling of warmth and protection from the rain that had now started its relentless pounding once more against the windows of the old hostelry. The wind howled like a demented banshee, and the Bantam was glad that he had found sanctuary in this pleasant inn.

The landlord was a small, fat, jovial fellow who looked as if he had stepped straight out of a Dickens novel. He had a mass of unruly white hair, ruddy cheeks, and a squat nose that looked as if it had been broken at some time, and a beaming smile that set his face alight.

The Bantam guessed (correctly as it turned out) that the Landlord was a retired farmer, as with a huge grin on his face he pulled a foaming pint of bitter, that had obviously come straight from the wood, and placed it on the bar.

Gratefully sipping his drink, Brian allowed his eyes to wander around the small cosy bar, taking in the old pine settle standing beside the fireplace, and the abundance of cast iron Britannia tables around the cosy room. Then his gaze halted and his face lit up with delight and astonishment. Nestling in the far corner of the bar was a corner cupboard. Not any old corner cupboard, but a large eighteenth century barrel fronted pine corner cupboard

It was magnificent!

It had a domed top that had been lovingly and beautifully carved from a single piece of pine. The gesso that had been applied to the door and the base was still intact and a dentil moulding nicely finished it off.

It was a craftsman's piece of furniture and he marvelled at the skill of the long dead carpenter that had created it. The two open shelves at the top held an assortment of modern plates and jugs that, to the Bantam's eyes, looked completely out of place.

'You should be holding a nice set of lustre jugs,' he murmured to himself as he took another sip of his rapidly diminishing drink.

He was so enthralled with the pine corner cupboard that he didn't notice the landlord come from behind the bar, until, in his lilting Welsh voice, he exclaimed, 'Bloody old cupboard. Don't know what the wife sees in it. It's too bloody big for this room isn't it?'

The Bantam's heart gave a double beat.

He would have expected the landlord to say something complimentary about the cupboard instead of running it down.

Maybe. Just maybe, there might be a chance that he would be able to buy it, and, with his thoughts racing, nineteen to the dozen, he slowly walked over to the bar to replenish his drink.

Brian spent the next couple of hours drinking at the bar with Selwyn, (for that turned out to be the landlord's name), and gaining all the information about the pine cupboard that he could from him. Selwyn, for his part, was only too happy to chat as the bar was relatively empty and the large tots of whiskey that Brian kept buying for him were very welcome.

It transpired that Selwyn loathed the corner cupboard almost as much as his mother-in-law to whom it had once belonged. After her death, the cupboard was passed on to her daughter, his wife, Gladys who was at this moment in time on holiday in Spain with a friend. Selwyn held the belief that she was there with another man. She had left him to run the pub single-handed for a fortnight and he was in a resentful frame of mind and kept referring to his wife as 'my bloody Gladys'.

As the evening wore on, the Bantam and Selwyn became very well acquainted. It's amazing how quickly friendships were formed when the whiskey was flowing freely.

Most of the customers had gone. There were just a couple of diehards left playing dominoes in the other bar. The Bantam decided that now was the time to make his move.

'Selwyn,' he said as casually as he could, 'how about selling me that old cupboard? I'll give you fifty quid for it. Cash in your hand.'

'Dew no bach,' Selwyn replied, quickly taking another sip of his whiskey. 'I can't sell it to you. My bloody Gladys would kill me if I did. Although I must admit, fifty quid would come in very handy. Business hasn't been so good lately.'

Brian knew better than to press the point, but he also knew that he had sowed the seed in Selwyn's mind, and that given time, and a bit of luck, that seed would germinate.

It was now getting late and, as the conversation progressed, it became apparent that Selwyn was not at all happy in his marriage to Gladys. Her going off to Spain was the final straw. He continued to run her down and Brian felt sure that her ears must have been burning wherever she was.

When closing time eventually arrived, Selwyn was much the worse for wear. He had consumed a vast quantity of whiskey and it was beginning to show.

Brian gazed again across the dimly lit bar to the corner where the cupboard stood gleaming in the flickering flames of the fire. For the umpteenth time, he made a determined vow to own it.

'Is it this quiet every night, Selwyn?' he asked making a swinging gesture around the room with his outstretched arm. 'There have been very few customers all evening.'

Selwyn reluctantly admitted that the business had been going downhill rapidly and the situation with Gladys hadn't helped at all as it had made him lose heart in the place.

Gladys seemed to be quite a headstrong, selfish person with no thought for her husband, or for the state of the business, Brian thought to himself as he took another sip of his drink.

It reminded him somewhat of his own mother who used to go on holiday to Italy every year with the profits from his father's shop. Unfortunately, his father (who he worshipped) was not a strong enough person to stand up to her, and eventually the business had collapsed. Brian, therefore, had a lot of sympathy for Selwyn and his problems.

'You are too good to your Gladys, Selwyn,' he went on recklessly. 'Do you know that? She should be here running the bar with you, not gallivanting around Spain with someone else. Who is he anyway?'

The die had been cast, and the Bantam waited quietly to hear what Selwyn would say, and if he would rise to the bait that had been carefully offered.

Selwyn sat down heavily on the pine settle, put his head in his hands and groaned out loud.

'Bloody Gladys,' he intoned in a low voice. 'Bloody Gladys,' and he rocked his head from side to side, tears starting to well up in his eyes.

'How about selling me the old cupboard, Selwyn? I'll give you sixty pounds for it.' Brian mentally crossed his fingers.

Selwyn removed his hands from his face and stared at the pine cupboard in the corner of the bar as if it was the cause of all the hurt that he had bottled up inside him.

The Bantam squirmed inwardly. 'Sometimes,' he thought to himself, 'you must use any method you can to achieve your goal,' but, as he admitted to himself, it didn't feel right. He really shouldn't be turning the knife in Selwyn's emotional wound.

Consoling himself with the thought that if he didn't buy it, then the knockers probably would, he waited and watched as Selwyn went through his emotional turmoil.

The room was cosy in the flickering glow of the dying log fire, the light reflecting on the old oak beams and the copper and brass that had hung undisturbed for years. Selwyn suddenly stood up and shook himself like a dog that had just come in from the rain.

'Sod Gladys and her bloody old cupboard. She should be here with me instead of living it up in Spain' and without more ado, he snatched the money from Brian's outstretched hand and stuffed it into his pocket.

He was still muttering 'Bloody Gladys, should be here with me,' as he sank back down onto the settle and put his head back into his hands.

The Bantam heaved a sigh of relief. The cupboard was his. He owned it now. He smiled to himself as he buried his conscience and started to remove the jugs from the cupboard.

He decided that under the circumstances he would forego his stay at the pub. It was quite possible that Selwyn would change his mind when he sobered up and Brian didn't want to be around when he did.

As the Bantam tied the cupboard to the roof rack of the Volvo, he gazed through the open door of the pub to where Selwyn was now fast asleep on the settle.

'Poor old Gladys,' he thought. 'She will have a fit when she returns to find the cupboard gone,' and he went back to the pub, carefully closed the door, and slowly drove away, a broad grin on his face.

The rain had stopped by this time and the moon was struggling to crawl from behind the clouds that were beginning to break up. There was a nip in the air, with the promise of a hard frost as the Bantam drove down the country roads heading for home, his prize securely fastened to the roof rack.

He didn't feel altogether happy about what he had done. True, he had paid Selwyn a fair price for the pine cupboard, but under what circumstances?

Would he have got it if he hadn't plied Selwyn with whiskey all night and got him into such an emotional state that he sold the cupboard just to spite Gladys?

The Bantam had a conscience!

Oh, how he was changing. A few years ago he wouldn't have cared less about Selwyn's feelings. In the early days he had no emotion at all when he conned his brother-in-law out of his grandfather clock.

It was unbelievable. He was finally developing feelings for his fellow man.

Chapter Seven

An Expensive Bureau

It was a bright sunny September morning and the sky was crystal clear as the Bantam climbed into the seat of the Volvo. There was a chill in the air, as if giving a warning that the balmy days of summer were quickly drawing to a close and that winter was just around the corner.

The chestnut trees were beginning to shed their leaves, and the local children were busy throwing sticks into the branches, to bring down the elusive conkers that hung tantalisingly out of reach on the upper branches.

As he drove slowly down the road, he could hear their cries of delight as yet another conker gave up the fight and fell unwillingly to the ground.

He thought about Ann and how one day he would be able to take her to the local woods to collect conkers and teach her the delights of nature.

Ann was almost a year old now, and although the Bantam would still have loved to have a son, he loved Ann with a fierce and overwhelming passion.

Alice had taken to motherhood like a duck to water, and as the Bantam admitted to himself, she did do a good job of it. It was true that they had quite a lot of arguments these days. Only that morning a row had developed over the fact that Alice had wanted him to look after Ann whilst she went shopping. This, as the

Bantam had tried to point out, was quite impossible, as he had to go to a sale and business must come first.

But as he drove through the sun kissed countryside, Alice's stinging remarks still rang in his ears, and it was with a great deal of effort that he forced himself to forget her, and concentrate on finding the farm sale that he had seen advertised in the local paper.

Eventually, after about an hour of searching, he found it He had followed the 'Farm Auction' signs that had been put up by the estate agent for miles down the twisting Welsh country lanes until he came across the rundown, untidy looking farm, nestling between two low hills.

Farm sales are a non-event these days, as stock is usually taken to the cattle market, and the furniture to the local auction room. But a few years ago a Saturday morning farm sale was a common occurrence.

The Bantam enjoyed going to farm sales, he loved the atmosphere as the local farmers dressed in their canvas jackets, green Wellingtons, and obligatory flat caps, strolled around the field assessing the farm implements that had been laid out for inspection.

He especially liked going into the barns, and the shippens, where the furniture had been usually brought from the farmhouse and placed around the walls for everyone to inspect. The smell of the cattle, and the sound of the farmers talking in Welsh would set the Bantam's adrenalin flowing as he made his way through the barns and outbuildings searching for the elusive piece on which he could retire!

He recalled one farm sale that he had attended a few years previously in which he had bought an old chicken coop, after dismantling it, he took it home, reassembled it and used it for a long time as a workshop.

He also thought about the Victorian pine dresser base that he bought for three shillings, when pine wasn't very popular, and had used, in fact still did use, as a workbench. It had three drawers across the top, drawers down either side, and a cupboard in the centre. The top was a thick solid piece of sycamore. Over the years drawers had gone missing, the cupboard door had broken off and it became scarred and misused. Had it remained in its original condition, it would have been worth quite a sum today.

He bought a cup of scalding hot coffee from the mobile canteen that always attended these functions, and made his way carefully across the muddy farmyard towards a distant shippen, from which he could hear the cattle bellowing with discontent in their stalls.

'It's as if they know that their home is being sold, and that they will be going to new pastures, or worse, to the slaughter house,' he mused, as he sipped his warming cuppa.

Thoughts of Alice and the row that they had earlier that morning started to crowd the Bantam's mind, and he quickly pushed them away as he cast his eyes anxiously around to see if he could see any other dealers.

He couldn't, but it would be a fair debt that they would be there, it would be too much to hope that he would be the only dealer at the sale. 'Although,' he pondered, 'it has been known.' Which was true.

A few months previous there had been three farm sales on at the same time, the Bantam had opted to attend the smallest of the three. Fortunately, for him, all the other dealers had gone to the larger sales, and consequently he had had a field day, and made quite a profit into the bargain. However, today was not going to be a repeat performance. As he made his way across the barns, he noticed Bob Anderson standing in the corner examining an old brass bound Bible. The Bible was sitting on the top of a scruffy looking Georgian mahogany bureau that, due to one of its back feet being missing, leant drunkenly against the wall.

His heart sank because he knew that Bob was the sort of chap that would go all out to get what he wanted. He had no scruples at all, and nothing the Bantam had done in the past could ever come up to Bob's unscrupulous standards. But, in the Bantam's opinion, Bob was a likeable enough chap in spite of a supercilious attitude that annoyed him immensely.

Aged about thirty, six feet tall, a thin face with a pair of piercing blue eyes that tended to look through you rather than at you, Bob Anderson looked the layman's vision of a successful antique dealer.

His head of thinning blonde hair was always perfectly groomed, and he spoke with a public school accent that had undertones of an Oxford or Cambridge education.

His parents owned a chain of hardware stores, in which he played an active part as a director on the board, in fact he was not really an antiques dealer in the true sense of the word, he was, what the trade referred to as, a dabbler.

Bob Anderson just dabbled in antiques. Much as he dabbled on the Stock Market only, it must be admitted, with a lot more success. This was not uncommon. Many people who had a bit of money to spare, and a love of antiques did this. They were frequently held in contempt by many of the dealers who relied on the antique trade as their sole source of income.

'Hello there, Bantam,' he called airily, waving his perfectly manicured hand in the air towards the Bantam, who picked his way carefully across the slippery floor of the barn.

Bob Anderson's patent leather shoes and perfectly tailored blue serge suit would have looked more at home in his director's office than in a scruffy Welsh farmyard, but it didn't seem to bother him.

'Not much here today, Bantam old boy,' he said in his plummy, far back accent that sounded quite alien amongst the Welsh that was coming from every direction. 'I don't know why I bothered to come really. Mind you,' he went on, turning to the bureau, 'this old desk might make a few bob, but it needs a hell of a lot of work doing to it. Anyway, coming out here to a sale makes a change from being stuck in a dreary old office.'

They spent a few minutes discussing the trade, and various dealers that they both knew, until Bob went to get himself a cup of coffee from the mobile canteen.

Brian smiled to himself and turned to inspect the bureau, as

Bob, gazing with distaste at a piece of cow dung that had somehow appeared on the surface of his patent leather shoes, walked slowly across the yard, rather like a man walking on hot stones.

The bureau was in a bit of a state, apart from the broken back leg, two of the drawer runners were broken and half the swan necked brass handles were missing. Plus the whole thing needed completely re-polishing. It was about two foot six wide, and as Brian pulled down the fall front, he saw a beautifully fitted interior, with a sliding base that when pushed forward revealed a hidden compartment. There was a small cupboard in the centre with wooden pillars one either side of it, and a mass of small drawers and pigeon holes. Along the top was a small carved frieze that when pulled forward revealed another secret compartment. It was really magnificent, and as the Bantam closed the fall again and placed the brass bound Bible back on the top, he knew that Bob Anderson, or no Bob Anderson, he was going to do his best to get his hands on the bureau.

It was not due to be sold for another couple of hours, so he made his way to where the auctioneer was starting to sell the furniture, after having sold the field full of farm implements.

During the sale he managed to pick up a few useful pieces, including a rather nice Victorian marble topped pine washstand that he knew would look lovely when stripped.

'That is,' he thought ruefully to himself, 'if Alf doesn't manage to break the marble, he's so damn careless it just isn't true.' And indeed it was true. Alf was the most clumsy, careless person that the Bantam had ever come across in his life, and he drove the Bantam to distraction. Brian consoled himself with the thought that he didn't cost him much, and after all, you only get what you pay for in this life.

By this time, quite a few dealers had started to appear on the scene, and the Bantam knew that the bureau would not come cheap, but he would give them a fair run for their money.

Bob Anderson, after returning from getting his coffee, stayed very close to the bureau, intently reading the old Bible, a fact that took the Bantam by surprise, it seemed so out of character. Interest in the bureau had increased, but Brian was not unduly worried as he knew that the repairs that were needed would put off a lot of people. He figured that it should make about eighty pounds at the most. With a bit of luck it would go for less. For his part, he would be very happy to have the bureau in his workshop, as it would give him tremendous satisfaction to work on it and restore it to its former glory.

The Bantam derived a great deal of satisfaction in knowing that after working on a piece of antique furniture, that over the years had been badly neglected, he could give it a new lease of life, and that it would be good for many more years to come.

Though it had to be said, that after working hard, lovingly restoring a piece of furniture, he often found it hard to part with, rather like saying goodbye to an old friend that he had grown to love.

He remembered, with affection, a seventy year old dealer who would always call in when he was on one of his regular buying trips. He had been in the antique trade all of his life, and would sit comfortably in an old crinoline stretchered Windsor chair by the warming pot bellied stove in the workshop, reminiscing about the old days. His father had been a coal merchant, and in the days of the great depression they used to exchange bags of coal for Welsh dressers or oak refectory tables.

Brian would listen avidly as the old dealer would return to his youth and his early days in the antiques trade.

The Bantam remembered the old man saying to him one day, as he sat by the hot stove. The grey smoke from his ancient pipe making a blue haze above him, his wrinkled weatherbeaten face intent with his memories.

'Bantam, my boy,' he exclaimed, in his slow deliberate manner, 'what we are dealing with here is not just old pieces of furniture, but living history, do you realise that?' he said, banging his hand down on the arm of the eighteenth century chair in which he sat.

'History,' he repeated. 'Living history.' And he pointed a nicotine stained finger at a small Georgian chest that stood in the corner of the workshop awaiting new handles. 'That chest was made in about seventeen hundred and fifty,' he enthused, 'when George the Second sat on the throne of England. Imagine what the world was like then. Imagine how many people have owned that chest, how many have lived their lives and then passed on whilst owning it, and yet the chest is still here.' His voice raised a little as he was carried away by his enthusiasm.

When the old man used to speak with such feeling to Brian about the furniture that he had for years taken so much for granted, it made him sit back and start to think.

He began to realise that the business that he was in was something very special, and that as the old dealer had pointed out, the furniture that he lovingly restored was a part of our heritage, and not just pieces of old wood.

As well as which, the old dealer had taught the Bantam a very important lesson in life. To be a good listener. Something that he had never been. But a trait that over the years he was to develop to good use.

At last it was time for the Georgian bureau to be auctioned. The auctioneer, dressed in a farm jacket and carrying a stick, walked into the barn and mounted a battered old milk crate that his assistant had placed on the floor before him.

'Now ladies and gentlemen,' he intoned, with a quick glance at the sheet in his hands. 'Lot number two hundred and fifty five. We have this very nice Georgian bureau. Where are you going to start me on this? Fifty pounds? Do I see fifty pounds to start me off? Come, come ladies and gentlemen, let's get started. Twenty. All right, it's a start. I am bid twenty pounds. Who will give me thirty?' and his eyes flashed around the assembled crowd as the bidding quickly climbed to seventy pounds.

The Bantam looked across the crowded barn to where Bob Anderson stood nonchalantly leaning against the bureau, nodding his head at the auctioneer.

The Bantam raised his hand and his eighty pound bid was quickly accepted. Bob Anderson nodded once more, his eyes fixed intently on the auctioneer's face. Again Brian raised his hand and the bid rose to a hundred pounds.

A soft voice spoke behind him.

'Bloody hell,' it muttered to no one in particular. 'That bloke with the blonde hair is determined to have it. He's nodding his head like a bloody nodding dog.'

Again Brian raised his hand. The price soared to a hundred and twenty pounds. Again Bob Anderson nodded slowly at the auctioneer, who by now realised that he had a battle on his hands.

The Bantam raised his hand.

The bid went to a hundred and forty pounds.

Bob Anderson nodded.

Brian realised that somewhere he had got things wrong, a hundred and forty pounds was more than enough for the bureau, but to his amazement the bidding continued climbing relentlessly up until it reached two hundred pounds.

Bob Anderson continued to lean against the Georgian bureau, seemingly quite unconcerned at the commotion that his bidding was causing the assembled crowd.

Brian was flabbergasted. There was no way that the bureau was worth that amount of money. Bob Anderson must be out of his mind. With a last slow look around, the auctioneer quickly brought his gavel down.

'Sold for two hundred pounds,' he said, trying in vain to keep the surprise out of his voice. A broad grin crossed the face of Bob Anderson as he gazed across at the Bantam and gave him a theatrical wink.

Brian couldn't understand it. Why had he paid so much for the bureau? Bob Anderson knew its worth as well as he did. Why did he go over the top like that? Pushing his way through the crowd to where Bob stood looking by the bureau with a broad grin on his face, like the cat that had just got the cream.

'You must be crackers, Bob,' he muttered as he finally got to

Bob's side. 'What the hell made you pay that much for it? We both know it's only worth half that.'

'That's all you know, Bantam old chap,' Bob replied, the inane smile still upon his face. 'Just hang on here a sec whilst I go and pay my bill. Take care of the bureau for me. I won't be long.' And he vanished into the crowd.

Brian turned to the bureau and had a good look inside it. What had he missed? He had seen nothing out of the ordinary in it.

Five minutes later, Bob Anderson returned to the Bantam's side carrying his receipt in his hand. Brian opened his mouth to speak and, with a quick gesture of silence, and a furtive look over his shoulder, Bob opened the bureau.

'This is the reason I paid do much, Bantam old chap,' he said, a broad grin splitting his face. 'It's really very simple.' As with another quick look around to make certain nobody was watching, he grasped one of the pillars a the back of the bureau and pulled it towards him.

The Bantam gasped in amazement. The pillar was in fact yet another secret compartment. As Bob tipped the pillar over his outstretched hand, a pile of sovereigns cascaded out, gleaming in the afternoon sunlight.

Brian was stunned.

No wonder Bob had paid so much. No wonder he hadn't left the bureau all through the sale. He was afraid that someone else might have discovered the secret. The Bantam felt sick to his stomach.

He had looked at the bureau.

He had just as good a chance to find the sovereigns as Bob had, but he hadn't been thorough enough in his inspection, and as the old adage so rightly says, 'To the winner go the spoils.'

Later, as he drove home, the Bantam felt very low. He had been so close to all that money and he had missed it through being careless, he could have kicked himself for being so stupid.

Once again he had learnt a costly lesson.

When he arrived home and opened the door to the shop, he

noticed that although it was beginning to get dark, the lights hadn't been switched on.

'Strange,' he thought, 'Alice should be in. Why are the lights off?'

When he walked into the kitchen he found the reason why. There was a note propped up by he electric kettle informing him that Alice had taken Ann and gone to stay with her mother for a few days.

That was all he needed. After the day that he had just experienced, he could have done with Alice going to her mother's. But there was more to come.

As he carefully went around the yard making certain that everything was locked up, he glanced into the stripping tank. There floating indifferently on the surface, was a small pine chest of drawers that was about to fall apart at the seams. A chest that Alf should have stripped while Brian had been at the farm sale.

'That bloody Alf,' the Bantam yelled out loud. 'I'll bloody strangle the lazy sod! He's forgotten to take the chest out of the tank. Just wait until I get hold of the stupid cretin.' With his eyes raised to the heavens in despair, he walked to the workshop to change into his stripping gear. He would have to strip the chest himself before it disintegrated in the tank.

It had just not been his day. What with not finding the sovereigns, Alice leaving him and Alf leaving a chest in the tank, he really felt that his guardian angel had deserted him for good.

Chapter Eight

The Davenport at Number 45

Alice stayed away for about ten days. Although Brian missed her and Ann, he was determined that he was not going to be the one to make the first move towards reconciliation. After all, why should he? He had not been in the wrong. It was Alice who had gone to her mother's in a huff. Let her make the first move.

Alf had been infuriatingly dispassionate about the pine chest of drawers that the Bantam had rescued, in the nick of time, from the tank.

'I thought you were going to take it out Guv,' he whined, casually picking his nose as the Bantam raved on at him.

'You bloody cretin,' he roared, getting even more incensed at Alf's complete lack of remorse. I should get rid of you right here and now. Don't you realise the value of the furniture you are stripping? Don't you realise that all this costs money?' and he waved his arm angrily in the air.

It was all to no avail. Alf was completely nonplussed, and Brian realised that he might as well be talking to the moon, as with a shout of, 'You stupid idiot!' he returned frustrated to the workshop.

Alice returned later that afternoon, as casually as if she had just gone down the road for some shopping, only Ann showed any sign that she was pleased to see her father.

A dog barked from somewhere behind the house as on the next day, in answer to a telephone call, the Bantam rang the doorbell of number forty five Albert Avenue.

He slowly gazed around the immaculately kept garden, at the weedless flower beds, the recently pruned rose bushes, and the trim freshly cut tiny lawn.

'Retired,' he thought to himself as he pressed the doorbell for the third time, hearing 'Home Sweet Home' chime faintly at the back of the house. 'You can always tell a retired person by the state of the garden.'

After years of calling on people, Brian had become an expert on judging people by the state of their gardens, and by and large he had found that if a person was retired, they have enough spare time on their hands to keep the garden neat and tidy. Not like the average working person, who was usually too busy to keep it up to scratch. He thought of his own garden and made a mental note to get Alf to mow the lawn.

As he waited impatiently for the door to open, his thoughts went to Alice. He couldn't put his finger on what exactly was wrong with her. Things were definitely not right. Although he had tried to sit and talk to her, it hadn't helped. Things were not the way they used to be. She was a lot quieter of late, and these days she never seemed to laugh or smile.

She had expressed a desire to get a part-time job at the local supermarket. Although it meant that Brian would have to take time to look after Ann, he readily agreed to her suggestion as he respected the fact that she wanted her own independence and some money of her own. But she never ever mentioned the ten days that she had supposedly spent with her mother, and quickly changed the subject if he brought it up. The Bantam had a lot to learn about women.

She also had a tendency these days to go to bed early, and to be, or at least appear to be, asleep when he wearily climbed into bed at the end of a busy day.

The thought crossed his mind that Alice might have got herself another man, but he quickly pushed the thought to the back of his mind as his stomach tightened at the very thought of it.

'No,' he thought, as he yet again pressed the doorbell of number forty five. 'The idea is too fanciful to be true.'

The door was eventually opened by a pleasant looking woman with a kind open face who looked, to the Bantam, to be in her early sixties. She had a mass of curly white hair, and a pair of pink spectacles rested on her nose.

'Sorry to have kept you,' she smiled sweetly at the Bantam, 'but I was out the back and I didn't hear the door bell going.'

'That's all right luv,' Brian replied, a broad smile upon his face, 'I understand you have some furniture to sell?' and with a slow nod of her head the lady stepped to one side and beckoned him to enter.

As it happened it was quite a disappointing call because the furniture that she was selling was mostly modern and quite unacceptable to the Bantam.

But with one exception.

Sitting underneath a large bow fronted window was the most beautiful Victorian walnut Davenport that he had ever seen. The sloping front was covered with the original green leather, and the intricately carved legs simply glowed with a mellow patina where it had been lovingly polished over the years. Four small drawers ran down either side, and the sun shining through the open window gleamed on the recently polished brass gallery that ran around the top. With the exception of one small little nick in one of the legs, it was in absolutely pristine condition.

'Is the old desk for sale?' he asked casually, his heart beginning to race a little faster in anticipation of her answer, as he admired yet again the design of the walnut veneer.

'Yes,' she answered with a smile. 'I am selling the Davenport. That's what it's called, you know.' Brian winced inwardly.

'It's Victorian,' she went on gaily, 'and it's been in our family for years and years. As long as I can remember anyway. My grandmother had it before that. It's very, very old.'

Brian just couldn't believe his luck when the lady said that it was for sale, and his hopes soared, only to be dashed to pieces a few seconds later.

'But I can't sell it to you,' she smiled sweetly at him. 'Oh no, I can't sell it to you. It's a family heirloom, and it has to go to auction. Anyway,' she prattled on, 'I wouldn't sell it to you, because you would only sell it again, wouldn't you? So by putting it in the auction we are bound to get more than you would give for it.'

His heart fell. Nothing that he could say would induce the old lady to sell him the Davenport. He even offered her three hundred pounds, which was slightly more than the present day valuation.

But to no avail. She was adamant. The Davenport was to go to auction.

'If it's worth that to you, it's worth more than that to me,' she went on, now becoming quite hostile towards him a she bundled him towards the door.

'Be off with you now,' she cried angrily, opening the front door with one hand and holding his arm with the other. 'I've heard all about men like you, frightening old ladies like me into selling their valuables.' And with a push in his back, she slammed the door.

He stumbled down the steps towards the front gate, treading in a pile of dog dirt that some uncaring dog had left behind, cursing as he did so.

Brian could not get over the old lady's attitude. Her hostility was unbelievable, and quite unnecessary. If she didn't want to sell the Davenport that was fair enough. She didn't have to get violent about it.

'Silly old cow,' he thought to himself as he scraped the offending mess from the sole of his shoe. 'I hope the bloody thing gets woodworm.' And he drove disappointedly away from number forty five Albert Avenue.

A few weeks later saw the Bantam at yet another auction. He tended to go to more and more auctions these days as it gave him an opportunity to get away from Alice, who was getting more and more unbearable as each day went on.

As he wandered through the rows of furniture, making a note in his book of the pieces that he was interested in, his thoughts went back to Bob Anderson and the incident of the sovereigns in the bureau. Bob had been bragging to all and sundry about it and Brian was sick and tired of the ragging he got about how he missed the sovereigns. He had also heard rumours of a trick that Bob Anderson had pulled with the bureau on a few unsuspecting dealers.

Apparently, he had got the bureau restored and had sold it to a dealer for three hundred and eighty pounds. A few weeks later he had returned to the innocent dealer and told him that he had a client who was looking for a bureau just like it, and could Bob take it to him and sell it, for a small commission.

The dealer readily agreed, and given Bob the price that he wanted for it, on the promise of the money that was to come. Needless to say, he never saw Bob Anderson, or the bureau again.

It appeared that Bob had pulled the trick a few times around the country with very great success. How true the story was, the Bantam didn't know. But knowing Bob Anderson, he thought it very likely that it was.

His thoughts were quickly brought back to the present by a light hand on his shoulder, and he spun round in surprise to find the laughing eyes of Brenda Evans gazing into his own.

Now Brenda was a mystery in the antique trade. She ran a large successful antique business sending containers to America and Canada. The Bantam had occasionally packed a container for her when she was short staffed and they occasionally borrowed the odd roll of cardboard when they were short of packing material. She had appeared a couple of years previously, out of the blue. Bought an old rambling farmhouse on the outside of town and started up in business.

She wore no wedding ring, but appeared to share the farmhouse with a young man many years her junior. She was about forty five years of age, petite, with an hourglass figure that any woman would envy. Her shoulder length auburn hair and sensuous mouth had the ability to send men crazy. She was, to put it mildly, a very desirable lady, as well as which she carried a lot of respect in the local trade.

'Hi Brenda. How are the boxes going?' the Bantam smiled, his pulse racing at the mere sight of this beautiful woman who stood before him.

'I can't complain, Bantam,' Brenda replied in a low husky voice that sent shivers up and down the Bantam's spine. 'I am short of a bit of gear to fill a box that must leave late tomorrow afternoon, to catch the boat. That's why I'm here today.'

Brian's heart sank when she said that. Brenda had far more money than he had, or ever would have for that matter, and if she was desperate to fill a container he was going to have no chance of buying anything.

Brian had always had a soft spot for Brenda, but being loyal to his wife, and unlike many other dealers, he had never attempted to let his feelings show. But the way things were going with Alice made him start to have second thoughts, and as he watched Brenda walk away into the crowd, she being oblivious to the stir that her voluptuous stride created, he wondered what his chances were of getting to know her better.

Suddenly he was brought out of his reverie. He stopped dead in his tracks. He couldn't be mistaken. It had to be the same. He quickly moved across to the piece of furniture and inspected the legs. Yes. There it was. There was no mistake. It was the Victorian Davenport from forty five Albert Avenue.

He gave a little chuckle, getting a strange look from the young man who was standing next to him. 'Well, well. So we meet again,' he murmured softly to himself. 'I wonder how much you will realise. With all the dealers here today, you should fetch a decent price. There's no doubt about it, you are a very desirable piece of furniture.'

Apart from the Bantam, there were about half a dozen dealers that he knew at the auction, and no doubt there were a few that he was unaware of.

At that moment, Paul Carpenter, an oak dealer that the Bantam knew slightly, came up to him. Standing closely, he put his arm round the Bantam's shoulder and whispered in his ear. 'Are you with us?' he murmured quietly, taking a furtive glance over his shoulder. The question took the Bantam by surprise, until it suddenly dawned on him what Paul meant. Then it hit him like a ray of sunshine through a cloudless sky.

'Yes, er, yes of course. Why not?' he replied, giving Paul a beaming smile. 'Of course I'll join you.'

'Great.' Paul grinned at him with a conspiratorial smirk. 'See you later on then.' Saying this, he disappeared into the crowd.

The Bantam was jubilant. After all these years he had finally been invited to join the 'Ring'. He could have danced for joy. He was recognised at last by all the other dealers as someone who was on a par with the rest of them.

Actually the 'Ring' as it is called, is completely illegal and frowned upon by all auctioneers. What happens is that all the dealers at a sale get together and agree not to bid against each other, consequently the furniture does not sell for as high a price (unless, of course, a private bidder runs the price up).

After the auction is finished, all the dealers that are in a ring get together and have a private auction between themselves, and re-sell the furniture.

If, for argument's sake, Brian bought a piece of furniture for fifty pounds at the auction, then at the private auction between the dealers it would then be sold to the highest bidder. If it made a hundred pounds, the difference would be split between the dealers. Many dealers who are in the ring, actually leave an auction having made money but not having bought a stick of furniture at all. It is hard luck on the poor vendor, who had put furniture into the sale, confident that it will reach its highest price, but in reality it will only reach a fraction of its true worth. The ring will get the benefit of it at their private auction later.

He glanced across the hall to where Brenda was warming her hands on a radiator. She caught his eye and gave him a broad wink, sending shivers down his spine. Now he knew why he had been admitted into the ring! It had been Brenda who had been the instigator of it. It had been her influence that had enabled him to be admitted without any argument.

He pondered on the prospect of a more meaningful relationship with Brenda as he watched her leaning seductively against the radiator.

'Ah well,' he thought to himself, as he pushed thoughts of Alice and Ann to the back of his mind, 'what will be, will be. Life usually has a way of working things out. If it's going to happen, then it will do.'

Without more ado, the sale commenced.

Brenda was doing most of the bidding, with occasional items being bought by other dealers (including the Bantam) to allay suspicions. About halfway through the sale, the Davenport from number forty five Albert Avenue came up for sale.

Brenda started the bidding off with a bid of fifty pounds, but a young man and his girlfriend who were standing just behind her quickly ran the price up to a hundred pounds.

'One hundred and ten. Do I see one hundred and ten pounds anywhere, ladies and gentlemen for this beautiful example of early Victorian workmanship?'

Brenda raised her hand once again.

'Do I see a hundred and twenty anywhere?' The auctioneer searched the room..

Reluctantly the young man standing behind Brenda raised his hand after being prompted by a dig in the ribs by his girlfriend, but with a nod of her beautiful head, Brenda raised the bid yet again. The young man prudently put his hands in his pockets, much to the disgust of the young girl.

'Is there any advance on one hundred and forty pounds ladies and gentlemen? Do I see any advance on one hundred and forty pounds?' and seeing no further protest, the auctioneer brought his gavel down with a loud bang.

Brenda winked at Brian, sending a shiver down his spine and he thought of the white haired old lady at forty five Albert Avenue. She would have a fit if she knew what a ridiculously low price the Davenport went for. She would be even more horrified if she knew that it would take pride of place in the private auction that was to follow!

The Bantam watched Brenda writing the price of the Davenport down in her notebook, a silver fountain pen held gracefully in her perfectly manicured hand. He felt a stirring in his loins and he looked forward to the private sale.

A couple of hours later found him, with all the other dealers, sitting uncomfortably in Paul Carpenter's Luton van, parked in a lay-by, surrounded by a choking haze of blue cigarette smoke.

The smell of Brenda's perfume washed provocatively over him as he sat next to her in the close confines of the van, making it hard for him to concentrate on the dealings at hand.

So far, he had done quite well. He had made fifty pounds and had held a nice little gypsy table. If he was honest with himself, it was more to make a good impression on Brenda than to own it, but in any case, he felt he could still make a profit on it.

Next came the Davenport. Referring to her notebook, Brenda declared the price that she had paid for it – one hundred and forty pounds. Brian Fisher, a dealer from Cheshire who was sitting on her right put ten pounds on it.

'I'll put ten on it,' murmured Paul Carpenter, and so it went round the ring until it finally came back to Brenda who held it at three hundred and twenty pounds.

'I want to keep it for myself,' she whispered in the Bantam's ear as she placed a warm hand on his thigh making the Bantam's heart race.

'I can tell you a story about that Davenport, Brenda,' he replied softly.

'Come back to my place afterwards for supper,' she whispered throatily, squeezing his thigh again, 'and you can tell me all about it.'

With thoughts of Alice having long since vanished, the Bantam readily agreed.

Later that evening as he slowly followed the rear lights of Brenda's Volvo back to her farm, his thoughts went back to number forty five Albert Avenue. After the saleroom commission was taken, the old lady would get about a hundred and ten pounds for the Victorian Davenport. He had offered her three hundred pounds. As events had proved, that was a fair price, but because of her greed, the lady at number forty five had lost out.

Brian, however, had had a very profitable day. Having left the private auction with over a hundred pounds in his pocket, and an invitation back to supper with a very charming and sexy lady. He felt very satisfied with his day's work.

'Which,' he mused as the two vehicles came to a stop in Brenda's drive, 'only goes to show that your local antique dealer will always give you the best price.'

Grinning at Brenda as she grasped his hand in hers, he was willingly led towards the house, his heart beating quickly in anticipation of the evening that they had ahead.

Chapter Nine

Whiskey Galore

The Bantam wasn't very happy. He sat mournfully in the shop watching the rain as it hammered mercilessly at the windows, as if trying to gain entrance.

Alice had gone for a walk, even though it was raining, taking Ann with her in her pushchair. She still wasn't talking to him, having not yet forgiven him for coming home at four in the morning after his long evening with Brenda Evans. The memory of which still sent his pulses racing when he thought about it.

He had told Alice that he had gone to an all night poker school with some of the dealers from the sale. He didn't think that she believed him for a minute, but he was slowly getting to the stage where he really didn't care any more.

He hadn't seen Brenda since that fateful night. He tried to ring her once, but a young male voice answered the telephone and he quickly put down the receiver.

Alice was becoming more and more unbearable every day. Even Alf had noticed that there was something wrong.

'The missus don't be too happy today Guv, do she,' he mumbled one day when the Bantam took him his morning cup of tea down to the stripping patch.

'What you want to do is buy her a bloody big bunch of flowers. That will see her right,' he said as he emptied the large mug of tea in two swallows.

'Christ, he must have an asbestos throat,' Brian thought idly, as he inspected a large pine wardrobe that Alf was stripping. He looked up from his thoughts to see Alf slowly chewing on a large Swiss roll, as contentedly as a cow chewing the cud. His pair of false teeth on a brick beside him. A look of bliss on his face.

The sight was revolting.

'Alf,' he said wearily, turning away in disgust. 'Tell me, why do you take your teeth out to eat? Most people leave them in. Why must you be different?'

'Well, it's like this Guv,' Alf belched and greedily pushed the last of the cake into his cavernous mouth. 'If I eats with them, I might get them broken, mightn't I?'

The Bantam turned away in despair at Alf's confused logic, and wearily made his way back into the shop to try and finish the newspaper that he had been trying to read since he had opened the shop that morning.

The rain continued to pour down. Brian threw down his paper in disgust, and brooded. It was amazing, he thought, watching the rain trickle in unceasing rivers down the window pane, it was amazing the unscrupulous characters that one came across in the antiques business. Bob Anderson re-selling a bureau time and time again was but only one example.

Take for instance, the ticket switch, and a grin came over his face at the thought.

Now the ticket switch can only be pulled off successfully in an antiques shop that is staffed by shop assistants, as opposed to the dealer himself.

The reason being, that in most cases the shop assistant has no idea of the price that has been paid for an article. Whereas the dealer would normally know exactly, and can quickly put a profit on without looking at the ticket.

The Bantam, although he was absolutely useless at remembering names, could tell you years after, how much he had paid for a particular piece of furniture.

What happens in the ticket switch is that an unscrupulous

dealer will walk casually into an antiques shop and browse around, looking carefully at the price tickets on the stock as he does so. When the shop assistant is not looking, he will surreptitiously change the price ticket from say, a clock that is priced at two hundred pounds, to a Loo table that is priced at three hundred pounds. The unsuspecting shop assistant, not knowing any different, sells the table at two hundred pounds and the dealer is a hundred pounds better off.

Price tickets, as a rule, are of the self sticking kind. Making it a very simple task to exchange them when the shop assistant is not looking. It has been known, for a dealer to even be taken in by this ploy on more than one occasion.

Another character that sprang to the Bantam's mind as he gazed gloomily out of the window, was the Dutchman. Now he really was a character. He used to come over from Holland about once a month to buy Victorian mahogany furniture, especially Victorian Loo tables.

On the occasion that he was thinking about, he had pulled up outside the Bantam's shop in a small canvas covered pick-up truck that was full to bursting.

Brian had groaned inwardly as he saw the large load. He thought that there was no way that the dealer could get another piece of furniture in his truck.

But he had been wrong!

The Dutchman bought a Loo table for a hundred pounds, carried it outside and quickly disappeared into the interior of his truck. He reappeared a few seconds later with a saw in his hands, and to Brian's horror, he nonchalantly started to saw the base off the table.

Brian could not believe what he was seeing. He was absolutely dumbstruck. As the Dutchman, quite unaware of the panic he was causing continued to saw through the base of the table.

When the Bantam questioned him about his actions, he explained airily that when he got back to Holland it wasn't a difficult task to drill a hole on either side of the base and insert a dowel. After gluing the two pieces together, nobody would be able to tell the difference and he could get much more on his truck by vandalising the table. As it turned out, in the years that lay ahead, the Bantam was to remember the Dutchman and use the same technique himself when he went on buying trips to Ireland for furniture.

Antique dealers are a strange bunch, he mused, as he let his thoughts wander. So are the privates, come to that. He smiled to himself. Take the business of the whiskey barrel, and he laughed out loud at the memory.

It had all begun about two months previously. The Bantam was in the shop bemoaning to himself about the state of the business, and nursing a hangover, caused by an overindulgence of Canadian Club the night before.

The doorbell rang loudly and he winced as a pain shot through his head. He turned to the door and found himself gazing into the most beautiful pair of grey eyes that he had ever seen in his life.

His headache disappeared like a snowball in a heatwave, and his heart went into second gear. Standing before him was the most gorgeous woman that he had ever seen.

She was about five feet four inches tall, young, (about twenty three he thought) and with a figure that would have put Venus de Milo to shame. Her long blonde hair gleamed in the sunlight that shone through the shop window. Her tight, provocative, silky dress that finished just below her knees, showed off her figure to perfection.

Her legs were a dream to look at, and the outstretched manicured hand that held a supermarket bag, showed the care and pride that she took in herself.

She enquired, in a low husky voice, if he would be interested in purchasing an old family heirloom, and opened the bag for him to look inside.

He placed his hand inside and removed a beautiful Victorian earthenware whiskey barrel, the like of which he had never seen before.

She explained that the whiskey barrel had belonged to an aged aunt of hers who had recently passed away. The young lady was emigrating to Australia and consequently had no use for it.

Brian had visions of her lying in the sun on Bondi Beach, and felt a stirring inside him.

'What do you think I should get?' she enquired innocently, and he smiled at her, his heart racing.

'How much do you want for it?' he asked slowly.

'You give me what you think I deserve,' she said and gave him a brilliant smile displaying a perfect set of teeth, and he wished that he could tell her exactly what he would like to give her. Struggling to keep his mind on business, he examined the barrel. It was about eighteen inches high, made of earthenware, with an unknown coat of arms embossed on the front. It had a small brass tap at the base and was in perfect condition.

Finally, after prolonging the interview for as long as possible, the Bantam bought the whiskey barrel for twenty pounds, which he thought was a very fair price to pay for it.

After he had paid her in cash for the barrel, it was with a great deal of regret that he reluctantly opened the front door of the shop and watched the young lady disappear down the street, her hips swinging provocatively from side to side.

He took a deep breath. 'Imagine being married to that,' he thought, as he placed the barrel on his desk. 'Christ, but she was fantastic. It's just as well that Alice wasn't in the shop when she called in. Although,' he thought to himself, as he sat down, 'the way things are, it probably wouldn't have bothered her anyway,' and he made a mental note to telephone Brenda Evans at the earliest opportunity.

He decided that he would keep the whiskey barrel. He took it upstairs to the flat and placed it on the centre of the Sheraton sideboard that stood in the far end of the lounge. It looked absolutely superb and he was well pleased with his purchase. Later that evening he showed it to Alice, hoping to get a positive response from her, but all she said was, 'Yes it's all right,' and walked slowly into the kitchen.

The whiskey barrel graced Brian's sideboard for about four weeks, until one Saturday night he invited some friends back to the flat for a drink.

Arthur Smith was a merchant banker from London and he and his wife were staying with some friends of the Bantam's who owned the local hardware store. They had been out for dinner and the Bantam had invited them all back for a nightcap.

Arthur was very interested in antiques and gazed around with interest as they passed through the shop to the spiral staircase that led up to the flat.

He spotted a small eighteenth century, brass dialled grandfather clock that stood at the base of the staircase. Its soft ticking giving an air of peace and tranquillity to the shop.

'I love the sound of a grandfather clock ticking, don't you dear?' Arthur's wife commented as she looked with interest at the clock, as it stood proudly, its patina gleaming in the lights of the shop.

'How much is it?' Arthur asked as he opened the clock's narrow door, to reveal the brass pendulum slowly swaying from side to side.

'A hundred and fifty pounds,' the Bantam coolly replied, having raised the price by fifty pounds on seeing Arthur's interest, plus the fact that he was a merchant banker.

'It's Welsh, you know,' he went on, 'made in a little village called Llansantffriad, up in the Welsh hills.'

'I wouldn't mind a grandfather clock,' mused Arthur as he ran his fingers over the polished oak, and Brian's hopes of a sale rose. Be could see Arthur's interest and he knew that if he played his cards right he could sell it to him.

Suddenly Alice's voice broke into the conversation. 'Come on up everybody and have a drink,' and she motioned them all up the stairs.

Brian threw Alice a look that would have frozen the door of

Hades itself. He was livid. He had been within an ace of selling Arthur the grandfather clock, and the silly bitch had spoilt it all.

'A hundred and fifty quid down the drain,' he fumed as he reluctantly climbed the staircase, 'and all because that stupid cow hasn't got the brains she was born with. Surely she could see that he was interested and that I could have sold it. Dear God, I don't believe that woman.'

Whilst the girls were in the kitchen making sandwiches, the Bantam played host and poured drinks out for everybody. Arthur gratefully accepted a large brandy and casually browsed around the room looking at the various antiques that were scattered about.

His face lit up with pleasure as he saw the whiskey barrel sitting proudly on the sideboard, and without further ado, he placed his drink on a nearby table and picked it up.

'How much Bantam?' he asked over his shoulder, as he lovingly turned the whiskey barrel over in his hands. 'What do you want for it?'

'Sorry Arthur,' Brian shook his head slowly, 'the barrel is not for sale. Not at any price.'

Every time that the Bantam looked at the whiskey barrel, he remembered the young lady that had sold it to him. He often visualised her lying on a sun-drenched Australian beach, and he could see her standing in the shop as it if were yesterday.

'It brings back too many memories,' he said, chuckling quietly as he gently took the whiskey barrel from Arthur's hands and replaced it on the sideboard. As he did so, he did not notice the look of determination that Arthur flashed at his wife.

'I'll give you fifty pounds for it,' Arthur said as he emptied his glass in one swallow. Holding it out for a refill added, 'cash in your hand now, no cheques.'

The Bantam got the impression that Arthur was used to getting his own way. His offer was also more than double what he had paid for it, but before he could open his mouth, Arthur spoke again. 'Sixty,' he cried, with a look at his wife, who nodded her head in agreement. 'I have a lounge with a long bar down one side and that whiskey barrel will look great on the end of it. I'll give you sixty pounds.'

Brian glanced at Alice, who, without looking at him, slowly shook her head and continued to sip her drink.

He thought of the profit he would make and he began to weaken. Why should Alice be so concerned? She didn't show any interest in it when he bought it up from the shop. So why should she bother now?

But Arthur was determined to have the barrel at any cost, so much so that he continued to raise the bid until it reached eighty five pounds. He walked across to the sideboard and once more lovingly picked up the whiskey barrel.

'Please, Bantam,' he begged, 'eighty five pounds. I really want it.'

But still Alice stubbornly shook her head.

'This is ridiculous,' the Bantam thought to himself, as he poured a large Canadian Club from the decanter on the sideboard. 'Eighty five pounds is eighty five pounds, when all is said and done. Why is Alice being so stubborn?'

He could se eighty five pounds going down the proverbial plughole, and he didn't like it one little bit. Alice didn't care about the money he would make on the deal. She was just being awkward to spite him.

'Bantam,' Arthur turned to Brian and put his hand on his shoulder, 'you are a hard man, so I will tell you what I am going to do.'

'What's that Arthur?' Brian replied, taking another sip of his drink. 'What are you going to do?'

'I want this whiskey barrel, and I always get what I want,' Arthur said quietly, holding the whiskey barrel possessively against his chest. 'I'll give you a hundred pounds, and,' he held up his hand to silence the Bantam, who had opened his mouth to speak. 'And not only that, I'll also have the grandfather clock downstairs for a hundred and fifty pounds.'

The Bantam's automatic refusal died on his lips, and Alice stopped shaking her head.

He quickly held out his hand. They say that every man has his price, and the Bantam had just reached his. Discussion with Alice, and the wrath that she would probably bestow on him could come later. He wasn't about to turn down that sort of profit.

'It's a deal Arthur,' he said quickly, slapping him hard on the shoulder, almost causing Arthur to drop the barrel. 'If you want it that badly, you can have it,' and he turned to Alice and threw her a malicious grin.

She gave him a look like thunder and disappeared into the kitchen carrying the empty glasses on a tray.

'Thank you Bantam,' Arthur said simply, and getting his wallet out of his hip pocket, he commenced to count twenty five ten pound notes into Brian's open hand.

Watching Alice's departure into the kitchen, Brian knew that the storm would burst later when their guests had departed. He knew, but he didn't care any more. He knew now that all Alice wanted was an excuse for a good row.

And he was right. After everybody had gone, Alice started, he ignored it. Reluctantly climbing into bed, he knew that before very long he was going to have to do something drastic about Alice. And the thought of it drove all the pleasure of the sale from his mind.

Chapter Ten

The House Clearance

The decision to do something about Alice was taken from the Bantam two days after Arthur Smith had bought the whiskey barrel.

She left him for another man.

The Bantam was absolutely devastated.

It seemed that for the past few months, whilst she had been working part-time at the local supermarket, she had also been having an affair with the Assistant Manager. He was going to leave his wife and set up home with her and Ann. Leaving not only the Bantam shattered, but his own young wife and two year old daughter as well.

Brian's stomach felt as if someone was slowly twisting a knife in it, when he thought of Alice in the arms of another man. He was the one that had always threatened to do something about the situation. But now that it had actually happened, he felt completely lost and alone.

He wandered around the empty flat, a glass of whiskey in his hand, feeling helpless and unwanted.

He picked up one of Ann's toys from the bedroom floor and a sob caught in his throat as he wondered if he would ever see his little girl again. He refilled the whiskey glass for the fifth time.

Maybe, he thought slowly as the whiskey started to take effect, maybe she was only kidding him. Maybe she had gone to her mother's just to teach him a lesson. But deep inside, he knew that he was just fooling himself. Alice had finally left him. He would have to face his Achilles Heel.

Being Alone!

He had a deep fear of being on his own. He knew that on his own he was completely and utterly useless. He had to have someone around him. Anyone, as long as he wasn't by himself. He could not stand the prospect of facing life without anyone.

But now Alice had gone. He was alone, and as the prospect loomed before him, he poured yet another drink, slumped down on the chesterfield and gave release to his tears. The Bantam wasn't crying for Alice. He wasn't even crying for Ann. He was crying for himself. After a couple of months had gone by, the Bantam was slowly coming to terms with the situation, and learning to cope on his own. He had heard through the grapevine that Alice and Ann seemed to be quite happy in their new life, but Alice had not been in touch with him at all.

Things in the shop were very quiet, to say the least. He had not had many calls lately, and his stock was getting rather thin on the ground. Unfortunately in the antique trade you can't just pick up a telephone and order a Welsh dresser, or a grandfather clock. You have to go out and search for them. There are several ways of doing this. You can advertise in the local newspapers, which is usually rather expensive. You can buy at auctions, which can be frustrating. You can go knocking, which is soul destroying.

Or you can have a house clearance.

A few years before, when the Bantam had first started in the antiques trade, if someone died, the local dealer would be called in to buy the contents of the house. He would clear everything out, and literally sweep the floor clean when he left. Nowadays, this isn't as rewarding as it used to be. Through instructive television, radio and magazine articles, the general public have been made aware that Aunt Sally's old furniture may not be a lot of old junk after all, but actually worth a lot of money.

Consequently families of the deceased, descend like a flock of vultures to pick the house clean. Leaving the dealer with the rubbish that was left, which was usually worthless.

But it is the unexpected finds that make the antiques business so fascinating. You never know what is going to turn up. Sometimes a call can be a complete waste of time. But others, as once happened to the Bantam, can be very profitable.

Brian always referred to it as 'THE' house clearance, and it all started when the telephone rang in the shop as he was sitting at his desk moodily gazing out of the window at the traffic that streamed past on its way to Hampden, a large town that lay a few miles further down the road.

The leaves from the chestnut trees across the street were being whipped up into mini whirlwinds by the cold north-easterly wind that was also causing a draught under the door of the shop.

The Bantam was very glad that he had had the foresight to light the portable gas fire, as its warmth made the shop very cosy, and the flying leaves outside could have been in a different world.

The shrill ringing of the telephone at his elbow startled him, dragging his thoughts, that had been with Alice and Ann, back to reality.

He resented the interruption and reluctantly picked up the receiver and placed it in his ear.

'Do you clear houses?' a female voice with a faint Welsh accent asked.

'Do we clear houses?' Brian thought to himself. 'Does a monkey like nuts?'

His attention now completely on the lady with the Welsh voice, he said quietly, 'Yes Madam, we clear houses. How can we help you?' and pulled a pen and paper towards him in anticipation.

It appeared that the lady's uncle, who lived in a little cottage, up in the Welsh hills, had recently passed away and his niece, Mrs Evans, who lived in the south of England had come to Wales for a few days to arrange for the clearing of the cottage so that she could put it on the market.

From her attitude on the telephone, Brian concluded that she was more concerned with getting the money for the cottage than anything else. She was the only relative and all the cash would go to her.

'There isn't a lot in the cottage, really. What there is, is just a load of old junk. But I want it emptying as soon as possible.' Mrs Evans went on and on about how she wanted the cottage cleared quickly, and Brian was relieved when she finally put the phone down.

He arranged to meet her at the cottage the following morning at ten o'clock, and later as he closed up the shop he looked forward in anticipation to his meeting with Mrs Evans.

The morning dawned bright and clear as the Bantam and Alf set off for the cottage which lay about half an hour's drive away.

Alf was very quiet. Ever since Alice had left the Bantam, Alf had gone quieter. It was as if he missed Alice and Ann almost as much as the Bantam did. The only comment he had made when Brian informed him of the situation was brief and to the point.

'It's your business Guv. Nowt to do with me.' And he never mentioned the subject again.

Eventually they found the tiny cottage situated down a long and twisting country lane. It was unkempt and run down and the small garden was a mass of weeds. The windows looked as if they hadn't been cleaned for years.

Mrs Evans looked exactly the same!

She was about fifty years of age, short and plump, with a hard face and blotchy skin that betrayed its owners love of drink. Her hair was untidy and didn't look as if it had seen water, let alone shampoo, for months. A half smoked cigarette hung from her thin lips, her eyes squinting against the smoke.

The Bantam was certainly surprised. From the sound of her voice over the telephone, he had expected to see a much smarter woman. 'It just goes to show how wrong you can be,' he thought as he walked up the narrow path that was only just visible beneath a tangle of weeds.

Mrs Evans struggled with the rickety door of the cottage, cursing it loudly until suddenly it gave up the struggle and opened with a loud crack causing her to lose her grip on her cigarette which fell to the ground.

She, unceremoniously, picked it up, replaced it in her mouth, and pushed the door back against the wall.

'Bloody door! The sooner this is finished with and I can get back home the happier I'll be.'

'You will clear it all. Won't you?' she asked querulously, turning to face the Bantam. 'There's not much, as I said. I don't expect you to give me much for it. I just want it out of the way, sell the house and go back home to my hubby. I've already informed the local estate agents and they have got someone interested in it. So it has to be done quickly.'

Brian, after quietly telling Alf to remain seated in the Volvo, walked slowly into the musty smelling cottage and wrinkled his nose. There it is, he thought to himself, the old familiar smell.

It was a funny thing. You could always tell if a property has been occupied by an old person. It has a peculiar odour all of its own. The Bantam had once been told by a friend in the medical profession that it was caused by the drugs that elderly people often took permeating through the skin.

How true that was, he didn't know, but he was inclined to believe it, as he had come across the odour many times before in property that had been occupied by old people.

The first thing to greet his eyes as he walked into the hall of the cottage, was a magnificent mahogany Victorian hallstand. It had a large bevelled edge mirror, set into the back, with a profusion of grapes carved all around the edge. Mahogany pegs ran down either side, and the base formed a seat. It was a beautiful thing. His heart leapt at the sight of it.

The hallstand, along with everything else in the house, was covered in a thick layer of dust. As he ran his finger through it, Mrs Evans quickly said, 'You must excuse all the dust. My uncle was in hospital for eight months before he died, and nobody has been in since he left.' She delved deep into her tatty handbag and triumphantly produced a crumpled packet of cigarettes, rather like a conjuror produces a rabbit out of a hat.

'Have a good look round, won't you.' She held a battered lighter up to her cigarette, 'I'm just going down to the post office. You work out how much you are going to give me for this lot. As I said, I don't want much. I just want the place emptied. I'll see you later.' And with a puff of cigarette smoke, she vanished through the front door.

The Bantam slowly pushed open the door to the front room and stood back in amazement. Before him lay a veritable treasure trove. The room had a black cast iron fireplace with an oven at the side. Heated by the fire, this oven was the usual method of cooking in these small cottages. A fender of solid brass skirted the front. This was flanked by a brass footstool, on which sat the finest copper kettle that he had ever seen.

To the right was an eighteenth century oak country made bureau, the patina glowing through the layers of dust and grime.

On the wall above, hung a beautiful double weight Vienna clock. Its two brass weights shining in the sunlight, that struggled through the grime covered windows, its prancing horse on the top still intact.

His eyes turned towards the bay window in which sat a Victorian mahogany wind out dining table, surrounded by four mahogany sabre legged Regency chairs, the upholstery of which was showing the ravages of time. In the hands of an experienced upholsterer though, they would be no problem. The Bantam whistled through his teeth as he viewed the dust covered furniture and looked around in the hope that he would find two more chairs to make up the set of six.

But in this he was disappointed.

He shrugged his shoulders with a grin.

'Ah well,' he murmured, 'I suppose you can't have everything. But a set of six would have been very nice.'

In the corner of the room stood a small oak square dialled

country made grandfather clock. The pediment was broken off and a piece was missing. He later learnt from Mrs Evans, that her uncle had shot it off in an accident with a shotgun. Fortunately no one had been injured, but her mother had fainted with fright.

The Bantam could not get over the furniture in the small room. Although it was dirty and it was obviously a long time since anyone had treated it with the love and care it deserved, it was still a marvellous find.

As he climbed the dark staircase to the upstairs rooms, he noticed a pair of lovely old seascapes painted on canvas adorning the wall. He was unable to make out the name of the painter, but they were very well painted indeed. The fine detail of the old sailing ships on the ocean with the sun setting in the background casting a golden glow over the sails caused him to stoop and gaze in fascination at them.

The first bedroom produced a nice little late Victorian three piece pine bedroom suite. A pretty pink and white Royal Doulton jug and basin stood on the small marble topped washstand, and the triple mirrored dressing table looked quite elegant in spite of the thick layers of dust. The walls were hung with old family photographs and Brian wondered what they would have thought of Mrs Evans and her selfish and uncaring attitude towards the death of her uncle, and her contempt for all of his beautiful furniture.

He entered the second bedroom and his heart skipped a beat. Standing by the tatty old single bed was another Regency chair! He quickly scanned the room, taking in the carved oak bedroom suite as he did so. Was there a sixth chair?

There had to be. There couldn't be just five. Please let there be another one. Six chairs were worth double the price of a set of four.

But where was it?

The Bantam searched everywhere for the elusive sixth chair.

Nothing.

Not to worry, he thought as he disappointedly descended the

old staircase. In the space of a hundred and fifty years, it has most probably been broken and thrown away.

'Are you there? Are you upstairs?' Mrs Evans' strident voice calling up to him, broke into his thoughts.

He gave her a smile as he greeted her at the bottom of the stairs. 'You're quite right, Mrs Evans. There really isn't a lot here. What there is has got quite a lot of woodworm in it.'

'You will clear it though, won't you?' She breathed gin fumes into the Bantam's face, and he realised that the Post Office had not been her destination at all. She had obviously been to the little pub he had noticed as he had driven up the road.

'You will get rid of it all, won't you?' she demanded for the umpteenth time. 'And when will you clear it?'

'Yes, Mrs Evans,' the Bantam said as he reached for his wallet. 'I will do it. I must admit I don't relish the task. Everything is in such a hell of a state. I'll clear it for you though.'

He hoped that he would be forgiven as he handed Mrs Evans a pile of notes, that was much less than the furniture was worth, but he consoled himself with the knowledge that she wasn't at all bothered about the furniture, and he most definitely was.

'By the way,' he asked casually as he lit Mrs Evans' cigarette for her. 'I don't suppose you know if there is another of those chairs anywhere do you? And he waved his hand towards the Regency chairs. 'They're not worth a lot, but it would be nice to have a full set.'

'Haven't got a clue, luv,' she replied, hastily pushing the wad of notes into her handbag. 'How my uncle lived with this little lot I will never know. Personally I wouldn't give it house room.'

'Anyway, here's the key to the cottage. You won't forget to give it to the estate agents when you have finished will you? The address is on the label. Well, I must be off now.' She took a deep drag on her cigarette and with a last glance around the room said, 'Thanks for getting rid of all this. It's a weight off my mind, I can tell you.'

'My pleasure,' the Bantam answered with a genuine smile. If

she only knew the real value of the contents of the cottage, she wouldn't be quite so happy.

After she had gone, he searched again for the missing chair, but to no avail. But he couldn't complain, the amount of furniture in the old cottage would well reward him for his day's work, and a lot more besides.

He couldn't get over Mrs Evans' complete contempt for all the lovely furniture. He was amazed that she didn't appreciate it at all.

The kitchen produced a lot of fine pieces. There was a pine farmhouse table, with a set of six splat back kitchen chairs to go with it. Against the far wall of the kitchen, stood a lovely old pine dresser complete with spice drawers and spoon rack. Every cupboard and drawer produced something of value.

He went outside and called Alf in from where he had been sitting patiently in the Volvo. 'I thought you had got lost, Guv. Are we going home now?'

'No Alf, my old mate, we are not going home. At least not yet. You and I are going to take all the furniture from this little cottage back to the shop, right now.' And he gleefully rubbed his hands together as a broad grin crossed his face.

'But why don't we go back and get the big van?' Alf scratched his head. 'It would be a lot easier.'

And he was right, as Brian well knew, but he was reluctant to leave his treasure trove behind for even a few seconds. So, without further delay, they started to load the Volvo. Alf still bemoaning the fact that it would have been easier to go and get the big van. As events turned out, they had to get the big van anyway, as there was far too much for the Volvo to carry in one load.

Brian felt a little guilty about the paltry amount that he had paid to Mrs Evans. He actually had a twinge of conscience about it. But he justified it with the knowledge that she would probably have spent it on booze anyway, so he might just as well have the benefit of it.

After a long struggle they finally finished loading all the

furniture into the van and as he slid wearily behind the wheel he had a sudden thought.

The shed!

There was a large, dilapidated old shed at the rear of the cottage and he suddenly realised that he hadn't bothered to look into it. He quickly raced round to the rear of the cottage to where it stood forlornly, in the unkempt yard. It was secured with a rusty old padlock and judging from the amount of rust on it had obviously not been opened for donkey's years. Quickly grabbing a piece of iron bar that was lying on top of a pile of old tin cans and rusty sheets of metal, the Bantam forced open the door and stepped inside.

It was dark and gloomy, and, as his eyes got used to the dark, he could see that the only occupant was a large old oak cupboard standing forlornly in the corner, thick with grime and partly covered by an old tin sheet.

But no chair!

His heart sank. He had been convinced that he would find the missing Regency chair in the shed. He took a closer look at the cupboard and as he dragged the rusty sheet of metal aside all thoughts of the chair sped from his mind. It was an early eighteenth century Press Cupboard. True, it needed a little restoration, but to the Bantam that was no problem at all. One of its feet was missing. The rats had been chewing at the bottom edge, and a lot of the handles were missing. But with a little work, he could restore it to its former glory.

He opened one of the cupboard doors, and froze.

The sixth chair!

'So that's where you've been hiding!' He laughed out loud as he pulled it gleefully from the old cupboard. 'I wonder how long you have been in there, and why you were put there in the first place.'

On closer inspection, it had one broken leg, which could be repaired without too much difficulty. Apart from that, it was fine.

It was a very contented Bantam that drove back to the shop.

The Luton van loaded with his magnificent haul. Alf sitting, at his side, chewing noisily on a large apple.

'If only I wasn't going back to an empty flat,' Brian thought to himself, as he negotiated the early evening traffic. 'Half the fun of getting a load like this is having someone to share the pleasure with. I certainly couldn't share it with this moron,' he thought to himself, glancing across to where Alf was now fast asleep and snoring peacefully.

The Bantam was very, very lonely. As he drove slowly home, he decided that he would sell the shop and find somewhere else.

He would start again. Away from all the old memories of Alice and Ann, and the many happy times that they had shared together.

It was time for him to stand on his own two feet. To forget the past.

To face life again.

On his own.

Chapter Eleven

Weighbridge House

It took the Bantam about six months to eventually find exactly what he was looking for, and, when he found it, it was purely by accident.

He had been on a call and was driving late at night down the main road that ran between two large towns, about ten miles from his home. The rain was drizzling, making it necessary for him to have the windscreen wipers on. He casually looked out of the window of the Volvo at the sadly dilapidated farm, that the headlights picked out of the gloom as he rounded a corner. Suddenly he slammed on the brakes, much to the annoyance of the driver close behind him, who mouthed curses at him through his closed windows. FOR AUCTION, the words on the notice board nailed to the front gate screamed out at him. He quickly reversed and slowly drove into the driveway that circled the old farmhouse.

'There is no way that this place is going up for auction,' he thought out loud, as he got out of the car and started to inspect the buildings by the pale moonlight.

The grounds were covered in stinging nettles and knee high weeds, as he struggled to get to the back of the building.

With a feeling of exhilaration. His heart beating a little quicker, he picked up a stick and started to thrash at the nettles that had laid claim to the grounds many years before.

This was it!

This was just what he was looking for. Deep down he knew that he had found his goal. He was completely oblivious to the rundown condition of the property. All he knew was that this farm was going to be his. It was perfect for what he had in mind. The driveway ended in a large courtyard. Facing the back of the house, to his left was a large double storey barn, and to his right was a huge stone built building that stretched for at least sixty five feet in length. Alongside the barn were about half a dozen corrugated iron buildings which (by the smell that still lingered), had at one time obviously been pig pens.

He was ecstatic. Auction! No way! He decided there and then that he was going to own the farm if it were at all possible.

Suddenly he heard a rustling at his feet. It sounded like two animals were fighting for their lives. 'It must be rats,' he thought as he instinctively raised the stick and lashed out at the moving weeds in front of him. Blindly, he struck out to the left and right until all was silent and the weeds were once again still.

Cautiously, he parted the undergrowth and the sight that greeted him made him feel sick. In front of him lay two inert bodies, but they were not rats. They were hedgehogs. The Bantam had just murdered two hedgehogs who were taking the opportunity of the moonlit night to make love.

He felt terrible. What a thing to do. As he climbed slowly back behind the wheel of the Volvo, he felt ashamed of himself.

For the next few weeks, Brian was very busy indeed. After inspecting the building thoroughly in daylight, he confirmed his feelings. He was going to own the 'Weighbridge House', for that was what it was called.

The name came about because at one time in its past three hundred year history, it had a weighbridge outside, and the local farmers would weigh their sacks of wheat and corn before taking them to the mill that lay further down the road.

The Bantam went to see the Estate Agents, who informed him

that if he put in a sealed bid, along with another interested party, who would do the same, the best man would win.

He thought that the bid would be around ten thousand pounds. So he put in a bid of ten thousand fifty pounds. That fifty pounds was the deciding factor.

The only problem was that he didn't have any money!

All he had was his shop and his stock. Half of which would go to Alice in the divorce settlement, which was about to go to court.

He was undeterred though. Come hell or high water, Weighbridge House was going to be his.

He went to the bank for a thousand pound loan, which he put down as a deposit on the property. That left him three months in which to get a mortgage. Considering the condition of the farm this was going to be no easy task.

So the Bantam (as the Americans would say) went for broke!

It would cost him a further five thousand pounds to restore the farm, which had to be done in order for him to get a mortgage. If he didn't do it in three months, he would lose his deposit, and with it, Weighbridge House.

Nevertheless, he went ahead, regardless of the risk. Employing a team of builders to restore the house and selling his stock to pay the bills bit by bit as he went along.

Three months and five days later, he stood in the lounge of his new home. He had only a hundred pounds to his name. No stock, deeply in debt at the bank, and the mortgage inspectors were due the next day!

If the mortgage inspectors said that the farm wasn't up to scratch, the Bantam would go bankrupt, but the gods were kind to him and his luck held, and he got his mortgage, and Weighbridge House, with only a few days to spare. His gamble had paid off!

Later on that evening he sat alone in the empty lounge of the farmhouse, perched on an empty can of paint, a glass of Canadian Club in his hand, contemplating what he had achieved. It was a still quiet night, and there was no sound of traffic passing outside to disturb his thoughts. He had made it. He had got what he wanted. Weighbridge House was finally his. As he gazed thoughtfully around the newly decorated room, he suddenly shivered.

He was not alone!

The Bantam knew that there was another presence in the room. It was an indescribable feeling. He knew that there was somebody standing behind him. He turned quickly.

The room was empty!

But the feeling continued.

He took a long swallow of his drink. He was afraid, and yet he had the feeling that someone was telling him not to be. Slowly he put his drink on the floor, closed his eyes, and tried to make his mind a blank. If there was someone, or something, he knew that this was the thing that he must do.

Without any warning she was there. Standing in front of him, not that he could actually see her physically, but he could see her in his mind and sense her presence. She was an old lady with white hair, dressed in a long brown dress. Her wrinkled face held a benevolent smile. She smiled at him, her arms outstretched in welcome. It was almost as if she was welcoming him to Weighbridge House and thanking him for restoring the farm to its former glory.

His fear quickly left him. He knew that his struggle to get Weighbridge House had not been in vain, and that the powers that be were looking after him in the shape of the old lady in the long brown dress.

In the months to come he never ever actually saw her, except in his mind. He felt her presence very often, so much so that he used to talk to her.

'Hi,' he would say, as he went to the new bathroom with its sunken corner bath and bidet in the corner. He had even had a telephone extension put in as he was fed up with the phone ringing as soon as he had settled himself into a relaxing bath and he was forced to race downstairs to answer it.

'How are you today?'

He knew whenever she was around, because the air would turn suddenly chilly. But he was no longer afraid. In fact he used to chide her out loud, saying 'Come on, show yourself. I know you're there.' Truth to tell, if she had materialised, he would probably have had a heart attack. But he gained a lot of comfort from her presence as she made him fell less alone.

She was definitely there though. This was proved one day when Ann came to stay for a few days. Since the divorce, Brian was allowed to see Ann whenever he wished, and after the completion of Weighbridge House, she came to stay with him.

She loved Weighbridge House, and would gleefully explore the outbuildings and sheds with the agile inquisitive mind of an active four year old child.

On one occasion she was so active, that the Bantam in an act of desperation picked her up and placed her in a large empty water barrel to teach her a lesson, and to stop her from getting under his feet. Much to her disgust. In the turbulent years that were to come he often had a little smile at the memory of Ann standing in the barrel unable to climb out, crying for him to release her.

One evening, the Bantam was sitting in his high backed leather wing chair reading an article on the restoration of antique furniture, when the door of the lounge opened, and Ann stood before him, an innocent smile upon her cheeky face. It was about five o'clock on a chilly November evening. Outside it was growing dusk, and he had lit a log fire in the large inglenook fireplace, that he had lovingly restored a few months previously.

'Daddy.'

The Bantam continued reading, because he hadn't heard her come quietly into the room.

'Daddy.' Ann placed her hand on his arm and shook him insistently, until he reluctantly dragged his eyes away from the magazine and gave her his full attention.

'Yes love,' he answered with a smile. 'What's the problem?'

'Who's the lady in the brown dress?' Ann asked with childlike innocence.

The Bantam started.

'Who's what?' he said, his attention now fully centred on his small daughter as she stood before him, her hand still on his arm.

'Who's the lady in the brown dress, Daddy? You know, the one I saw in the big shed outside. I was playing in the shed and she came and stood beside me. She smiled at me. Then she went away. Who is she?'

It was then that Brian knew that the old lady was not just a figment of his imagination. She was real. She was here. Ann had actually seen her.

Ann was not the only one to see her. A few months later, a lady friend, who he became very closely involved with, also saw her. But Brian never did, but he knew that she was always there, and it gave him a great feeling of comfort to know that although he was lonely, he wasn't actually on his own.

Yes, the Bantam was lonely. He desperately missed Alice, and although he got a lot of comfort from Ann, it wasn't the same as the loving arms of a companion around him, or the gentle words 'I love you', whispered in his ear.

So he turned to work, and with the hundred pounds that he had left after restoring Weighbridge House, he managed to get back on his feet.

It was a hard struggle. The one thing that he had learned, was that if you are down, there is nobody around to pull you up, but there are plenty who are quite willing to push you further down into the mire, if given the chance.

He remembered when John Adams had once said to him, 'Bantam, Ireland is the place to go for pine. Go to Ireland.' So with John's thoughts in mind, the Bantam decided that he would take a trip to Ireland, and see what he could find.

It was to be an unforgettable experience.

Chapter Twelve

Across the Irish Sea

She was a very attractive young lady, about twenty five years of age, wearing a pair of faded blue jeans with a white blouse under a pale pink sweater. Her hair was as black as a raven's wing and her eyes of the most brilliant blue that the Bantam had ever seen.

Her pretty face was slowly turning green at the motion of the ship, and he gave her a slow smile of understanding.

'Rough, isn't it love.' He smiled again.

She looked desperately at him, and as the ship gave another lurch, she clapped her hand to her mouth and made a desperate dash for the side of the ship.

It was a particularly rough crossing. The Irish sea was tossing the ferry up and down with contempt, and a veritable gale was howling across the deck, threatening to hurl the Bantam overboard at any moment.

He was glad that he didn't suffer from seasickness, as the unfortunate young lady yet again leant out over the side giving in to her nausea.

But Brian was in his element. He loved the rough sea. Never ceasing to be amazed at the fury of nature at its angriest. Nevertheless, he decided that you can have too much of a good thing, and decided to make his way down to the bar. As he walked down the broad staircase to the lower deck, hanging on grimly to the handrail, he reflected on the purpose of his trip.

He had heard that as well as there being a plentiful supply of pine furniture in Southern Ireland, there was also a lot of mahogany. He had found out that there were differences between Irish and English pine, and looked forward to seeing it for himself.

Apparently the Irish pine furniture tended to be constructed differently from the English. It was far more decorative, with slanting slats in doors, as opposed to the English use of a flat panel, and carved pierced mouldings.

It also had a reputation for woodworm. This he found out to his cost, as when he was loading a pine dresser onto the roof of the Volvo, half the moulding crumbled away to dust in his hands. The woodworm in Ireland was really a problem and one had to be very careful of it.

A few hours later, the ferry finally docked at Dublin, and the Bantam drove on to Irish soil for the first time in his life.

His first job he thought to himself was to find a local antique dealer. He then could point him in the direction of other dealers in the area. That way he should be able to find his way around.

Typically of the Bantam though, ten minutes after driving carefully off the ferry, he was lost. He must have taken a wrong turning and now he had no idea of the direction he was going in, let alone the way, to Dublin. He spied an old, scruffily dressed, man walking slowly down the road, pushing an even older bicycle. The old man had an expression of sheer determination on his face as he wearily pushed the battered old bike along, chewing on a well worn pipe clenched between his yellowed decaying teeth.

Brian couldn't understand why on earth he didn't ride the bike. Still, they say the Irish are thick, perhaps it's true he thought as he slowed down.

Pulling up alongside the old man he wound down the window.

'Excuse me, Sir,' he smiled. The old man gazed vacantly at him, and stopped.

'Excuse me,' he repeated in a louder voice, in case the old man was hard of hearing. 'Can you tell me the way to Dublin, please?'

The old man continued to stare vacantly at him. Then, slowly taking his pipe from his nicotine stained lips and placing it in the pocket of his dirty tweed jacket, replied. 'Dublin is it, you say?' He spoke in a soft Irish lilt. 'Dublin,' he repeated, much to the annoyance of the Bantam.

'Yes, yes!' Brian was getting quite impatient by this time, 'Dublin. Which way is Dublin?'

'Well now,' the old man rubbed his hand across his unshaven face, 'if I was going to Dublin, I wouldn't be going from here.'

Brian stared at him in disbelief. 'But I am going from here.' His voice rose an octave in frustration. 'I am going to Dublin from here. From right here.' And he pointed to the ground to emphasise the face.

'I wouldn't be going to Dublin from here,' the old man mumbled, shaking his head. Then he just turned and walked away, still pushing his bike down the road.

The Bantam couldn't believe it. The stories that were told about the Irish were true.

About an hour later, after he eventually found his way to Dublin and booked into a rather nice three star hotel that he discovered tucked away down a side street. He had another opportunity to experience the eccentricities of the Irish. After booking in and signing the register, the desk clerk rang the bell and beckoned to a porter, who came over to the Bantam a broad smile on his jovial face.

'Follow me Sir,' the young porter said pleasantly, as he lifted the Bantam's heavy suitcase with effortless ease. 'Follow me and I'll be right behind you.'

Brian chuckled to himself as he dutifully followed the porter up the winding staircase that led to his room. 'It's true,' he thought, 'they are all crackers in Ireland!'

Later that evening as he sat consuming innumerable Irish hot toddies which were a speciality of the house, he found, thanks to the effort of the hall porter, the location of an antique dealer in Dublin.

The next morning Brian set out full of anticipation to meet a dealer called Paul O'Brien who dealt exclusively in antique pine furniture. According to the hall porter, Paul O'Brien was just what Brian was looking for. Brian hoped that he was right.

It was a cold December morning, and the sky was full of the promise of snow as the Bantam negotiated the early morning traffic, and headed for Paul O'Brien's shop which was in a small village about twenty eight miles away.

The Irish countryside was quite beautiful with its rolling green fields and Brian mused to himself as he drove, that it would look absolutely lovely in the spring, when the blossom started to appear and the daffodils showed their yellow nodding trumpets.

He found Paul O'Brien without too much trouble. Paul turned out to be a middle aged, short, stocky chap with a mop of black hair. His girth betrayed a fondness for Guinness (Liffy water, he called it), and had developed into quite a paunch. Brian wondered when he had last seen his feet, let alone anything else!

The Bantam explained to him that he had come over from England especially to find pine furniture, and Paul made him very welcome and ushered him into a large barn situated down a long path and right in the middle of a small field at the bottom of the garden.

'Help yourself,' he grinned from ear to ear, revealing a mouth full of black, decaying teeth. 'I'll be in the house if you want me,' and without further ado, he disappeared back up the path and into the house.

The Bantam stared in amazement at the pile of pine furniture that greeted him. He walked into the cavernous building that looked at first sight to be an Aladdin's cave of furniture.

It was about sixty feet long, and about twenty feet across. It was stacked almost to the ceiling with pine furniture. The Bantam opened his mouth in silent amazement.

The furniture was scattered about. Items piled high upon each other. It looked as if it had been just thrown in. Food cupboards on top of dressers. Chairs on top of tables. A complete muddle of furniture.

The Bantam knew that what he was looking at was a lot of moneys worth of furniture. It might be thrown without apparent concern into the barn, but he was sure that Paul knew exactly what was there, and in this he was proved right.

Disappointingly, on closer inspection, he found (after risking life and limb by climbing over the tangle of furniture), that a lot of it was either damaged, had pieces missing, or was full of woodworm.

The thing that really amazed him was the bright colours that the furniture was painted. Bright blue, red, yellow. All the colours of the rainbow. How anyone could live with furniture that colour the Bantam couldn't comprehend.

After about an hour, climbing over everything, he eventually found a couple of sycamore topped kitchen tables, and a set of four splat backed kitchen chairs, which after calling Paul from the sanctuary of his kitchen, he bought for a reasonable price.

It was then that he remembered the Dutchman's trick outside the old shop, and cursed himself for not bringing a hammer with him. It would be a simple enough job to take the furniture apart and reassemble it when he returned home.

'Paul,' he said, turning to face Paul O'Brien, who was busy wiping the traces of his breakfast from his face. 'Have you got a hammer that I could borrow?'

Paul looked at him with complete and utter astonishment.

'A hammer?' he said in disbelief. 'A hammer. What now would you be doing with a hammer?' But he went off to his workshop shaking his head in amazement at the strange request, and returned with a large claw hammer clutched in his hand. He watched open mouthed as Brian proceeded to knock the two pine tables apart until they were reduced to a few pieces of timber, which, with a broad grin on his face, he placed in the back of the Volvo.

'Well, bless my soul!' Paul said, 'What a thing to do.' And he slapped his hand on his knee and laughed so much until the tears ran down his cheeks.

'You're from Wales, you say,' he said with a grin, wiping away the tears. 'Well all I can say is that the Welsh must be as clever as the Irish. Holy Mother of God. But I have never seen such a thing before.'

'Come you now,' he added, as the Bantam returned the hammer to him. 'A man as clever as you deserves a touch of the Poteen,' and with another loud laugh, he put his arm around Brian's shoulders and led him back into the house, his shoulders shaking with silent laughter.

'Poteen?' the Bantam asked innocently, as he paid Paul for the furniture that he had just vandalised.

'Poteen, what's that?'

Paul stopped and turned to him, a look of horror on his face.

'Do you mean to tell me that you don't know what Poteen is?' He stared at the Bantam with as much disbelief as if he had asked him who was the Pope.

'You don't know what Poteen is? Well, well, maybe the Welsh aren't so clever after all,' and he laughed.

'Poteen, my Welsh friend,' he exclaimed slapping his hand hard on Brian's shoulder, 'Poteen is the Good Lord's own gift to the Irish. Come laddie, it's time that you were educated.'

In the large gaily painted kitchen, Paul thrust a large glass of what looked like water into the Bantam's hand.

'Drink that,' he said with a grin. 'It will put hairs on your chest. Go on laddie, straight down with it.'

Brian viewed the glass of liquid with some trepidation. He swallowed half the contents in one go, and choked and spluttered as he tasted it. It was like a mixture of nitric acid and turpentine, and when it hit his stomach, it just sat there and burned. He had never tasted anything so volatile in his life.

The nearest equivalent that he had ever tasted was tequila,

which he tasted in Mexico. But this was much stronger, and after a few more mouthfuls he found it quite palatable.

'What do you think of it?' Paul asked, as he downed a glassful in one swallow. 'It's made from potatoes. I brew it myself in that shed at the bottom of the yard.' And he waved his grubby hand towards a small shed that Brian hadn't noticed, nestling alongside the large 'pine' barn.

'Here,' Paul bent down under the kitchen sink and produced a large demijohn full of the potent mixture.

'Take this with you, but whatever you do, don't let the Customs men find it because it is illegal and you can be heavily fined if you are caught with it.' On this warning note, he thrust the large bottle into Brian's hand and burst into peals of laughter.

The Bantam left Paul O'Brien with the promise to return on his next trip, and, with the large glass of Poteen still nestling in the pit of his stomach, glowing like a fire of red hot coals, he bade him farewell.

Paul had directed him to a dealer called John Evans who was situated about thirty miles away and with the aid of a map, he found him without too much trouble.

John Evans, as it turned out, was English. He married an Irish girl a few years before and had come to live in Ireland.

With his long blonde hair, and blonde moustache, he reminded Brian of a young General Custer. He was in his late thirties, with deep blue eyes, and a smile that never seemed to leave his face, and when he explained who he was, and what he was doing, John immediately invited him to say for lunch. As the Bantam had not eaten since leaving the ferry, and with the effects of Paul O'Brien's Poteen still in his stomach, he readily agreed.

Over lunch, he related his encounter with Paul O'Brien. John laughed as he listened to Brian's encounter.

'Paul makes the finest Poteen in the whole of Ireland,' he said, his blue eyes twinkling in amusement. 'He's well known for it. But take care, what he said is true. If you are caught with it, you are in trouble.'

Brian was disappointed. It looked as if the Poteen of Paul's could cause him a lot of headaches, but he really wanted to take it back home with him.

Actually, what he really wanted, was to give Alf a glass of, supposedly, water and watch his face as he swallowed it. John suddenly broke into his thoughts.

'The thing to do Brian,' he said thoughtfully, a little grin creeping across his face, 'is to empty your windscreen washer of water, and fill it with Poteen. That way you will be able to get it through.'

This the Bantam did, and with success. So much so that on further trips to Ireland, he even took Ann with him, and on returning through Customs, gave her a large bottle of lemonade to carry on her lap, with strict instructions not to drink it. Not even to open it!

After lunch, John and Brian went round John's warehouse to see his stock, which was quite impressive, but not as much as Paul O'Brien's.

He saw a pretty stripped Irish dresser that he would have liked to put in the kitchen at Weighbridge House, but unfortunately John had decided that he was going to keep that particular piece for himself, and no amount of persuasion on the Bantam's part would make him change his mind.

Then he saw the table. All thoughts of the dresser disappeared from his mind, as quickly as snow on a hot stove. It was an eighteenth century farmhouse table, about eight feet long, with six bulbous legs, and stretchers all the way round. The stretchers had worn thin with decades of countless numbers of feet rubbing against the timber. The two inch thick sycamore top was pitted and worn through hundreds of years of constant use.

But it was painted a horrible bright blue!

John laughed at the expression on the Bantam's face, as he viewed the table with horror.

'Brian,' he grinned, 'one thing you must realise about the Irish is that they are like magpies. They like bright colours. It's not unusual to see a pine dresser painted all the colours of the rainbow.'

The Bantam took a coin from his pocket and scraped away some of the paint that lay thickly on the surface. Underneath, the honey coloured sycamore shone through the paint like a ray of sunshine through a cloudy sky as if willing him to remove all the layers of paint, so that once more it could return to the natural colour that its maker had intended all those years ago.

'How much,' he turned casually to John, trying hard not to show his enthusiasm. 'How much is the table?'

'Well now,' John rubbed the stubble on his chin, a thoughtful expression on his face. I was going to strip it, but let's face it, you have come a long way and you have already bought quite a bit of gear from me. You can have it for fifty pounds,' and he slapped Brian jovially on the back.

Brian couldn't believe his luck. Fifty pounds, it was nothing. Stripped and waxed, the table would make at least three hundred, and this table alone would make his trip to Ireland worthwhile.

They sealed the bargain and returned to the warmth of John's cosy kitchen to partake of the inevitable hot toddy, which by now the Bantam was beginning to get used to, and if truth be known was getting quite fond of.

The time had come for Brian to move on, and John, like all the other dealers that the Bantam came across in Ireland, watched in amazement as he casually knocked the furniture to pieces, with the aid of a wooden mallet borrowed from John's workshop and carefully packed them into the car.

By the time he had finished, his Volvo looked as if he had obtained a load of firewood on his trip to Ireland, instead of a lot of valuable antique furniture. It was with a lot of laughter and good wishes that he said farewell to John and his wife and promised to call and see them on his next trip.

The Irish countryside was beautiful as he drove slowly to the ferry that would carry him back to England. He drove past the large peat bogs and stopped for a moment to watch in fascination as the large cutting machines relentlessly ripped up the ancient peat, that had lain undisturbed for thousands of years, slowly maturing, like a good whiskey, only to go up in flames at the hand of man.

As he drove back to Dublin, his thoughts full of the marvellous pieces of furniture that he had found, a large wagon full of sugar beet passed him on its way to the processing factory where it would be turned into sugar and its residuals. He smiled to himself as he wondered how many people realised where the sugar in their morning coffee came from.

Driving along, he noticed large chunks of peat scattered on the roadway, and he stopped to pick them up. He had heard all about the burning qualities of peat, and the pleasant aroma that it gave off, and he wanted to try it for himself when he returned to Weighbridge House. It would be interesting to see if it was as good as the Irish said it was.

After about half an hour spent picking up the peat, he wondered where it had all come from. When he rounded the next corner, his question was answered. In front of him, driving slowly down the road, was a large tractor. The trailer that it was towing was piled high with peat, and every time it hit a bump (which was very often on the Irish roads), a few pieces would fall off, only to be eagerly picked up and added to the growing supply in the Volvo.

By now Brian was tired. He had had a good day. He was loaded with furniture and had met a couple of nice people. The next time he would come over to Ireland for longer. He had he whole of Southern Ireland to cover yet.

As he drew near to the docks, he decided that he should rearrange the load of furniture in the back of the Volvo. It looked ridiculous, like a load of firewood topped by scores of pieces of peat. It looked as if he was going to a bonfire. Not to mention the windscreen washer container full of illicit Poteen, along with countless lemonade bottles that he had filled with Paul O'Brien's potent brew. As he rearranged the load, he mentally kept his fingers crossed that he would not be stopped.

As it turned out, the Customs were no problem at all.

The Customs officer raised his eyebrows when he looked into the back of the Volvo and saw all the gaily painted wood piled high in the back, topped with a layer of rich brown peat.

'Oh, it's all right,' the Bantam said brightly, in answer to the officer's query about the wood. 'I am doing up an old house (which actually was almost true), and I need some old timber and there's no doubt about it, you can't beat good old Irish pine!'

The Customs officer scratched his head in bewilderment and waved him through, wondering for the hundredth time why he had ever taken the job as a Customs officer.

The Bantam secure in the knowledge that he actually had on board a large quantity of valuable antiques, on which he had not paid any duty, plus a lot of Paul O'Brien's illicit Poteen, laughed to himself, and pointed the Volvo in the direction of Weighbridge House.

But as he drove home through the rain that was slowly starting to fall, the exhilaration of his trip to Ireland began to fade. True, he had had a good trip. It had been a lot of fun. Most importantly, he had made a good profit on the trip. But he was going back to an empty house. He had nobody that he could recount his trip to Ireland to, except maybe, the old lady in the brown dress, and he might as well talk to a brick wall as talk to her, for all the good it did.

As he drove through the Welsh countryside bathed in watery moonlight, he wondered to himself where it would all end. He was so lonely, the feeling ate at his inside like a cancer, and the pleasure of his trip slowly faded away to be replaced by an aching inside him. He opened a bottle of the 'lemonade' that lay on the seat beside him and took a mouthful. As Paul's nectar coursed through his body, making a glow like molten lava running down the side of a volcano, he made a vow to himself. He would win!

No matter what the world threw against him, the Bantam would survive. And he would win!

Two hours later, as he turned into the driveway of Weighbridge House, he fancied that he saw the old lady standing at the window, as if waiting for him to return.

But it was probably only his imagination.

Chapter Thirteen

The Oil Painting

Alf wasn't happy.

Ever since the Bantam had moved from the shop to Weighbridge House, he had become decidedly unhappy.

'I wasn't employed to knock down brick walls,' he moaned s he demolished he old pig pens to make a large stripping patch.

'I'm here to strip furniture, not knock down walls.'

Brian grinned at Alf. 'Look at it this way, Alf old son,' he said condescendingly, 'if you don't knock down these walls, we won't be able to get in a stripping tank. And if we don't get in a stripping tank, you can't strip furniture. And if you can't strip furniture, you are out of a job. Right!'

Alf scratched his head, looked around at the pile of bricks and dust that lay scattered around him and said 'Well, yes Guv, if you put it that way I suppose you're right. But when am I going to start stripping?' He scratched his head again in complete incomprehension, as he picked up his lump hammer and proceeded to knock down another wall of the pig pens.

Brian chuckled to himself. 'I just hope that the old lady doesn't make herself known to him,' he thought. 'If she does, poor old Alf will run a mile.'

As he left Alf and returned to the house to get his coat, he mused on the fact that it was strange that he had never seen the old lady, only felt her presence. 'Maybe one day I'll see her,' he thought.

Business had been very good, and he decided that he would take a two day buying trip down into South Wales to see what he could find. It was a while since he had been in that direction. In fact, not since his trip to Ireland, and the purchase of the blue painted sycamore topped table, which was about three months ago. He remembered how nice the table had looked after he had stripped it. In fact it was only in the shop a week before he sold it.

He planned to take the coastal road, returning by the inland route. This would give him about twenty dealers to call on.

Including Rose.

Now Rose had been a very special lady to the Bantam, especially since Alice had left him. After Alice's departure, he had had a few lady friends, but nothing permanent. Although he really wanted a meaningful relationship, he was scared that it would finish up the same as his marriage to Alice.

Rose was as near as he had come.

She was thirty four years old, with long auburn hair, green eyes, a smile always on her pretty face, and a stunning figure guaranteed to turn men's heads. The only problem was that she was aware of this fact, and used it to her advantage.

She had been widowed for about four years. Her husband, also an antique dealer, had been killed in a rather nasty road accident whilst in the company of another woman. Unbeknown to Rose, they had been having an affair for years, and although the experience had left Rose a very wealthy woman, it also left her very bitter, and distrustful of men.

Brian and Rose had spent many memorable hours together in the past. Wining and dining and generally enjoying themselves and they had become quite close.

Unfortunately Rose had started to mix business with pleasure, by putting pressure on him to reduce the price of articles that she wanted to buy. So, reluctantly, he ended the affair, because to

Brian, business came before pleasure, and the two should never be mixed.

Smiling quietly to himself as he thought of Rose and the times they had enjoyed together, he headed south through the busy morning traffic, a smile on his lips and full of optimism.

One of the pleasures of a buying run is the uncertainty. You never know what you are going to come across at your next call Perhaps you will know the value of an article and the dealer will not, perhaps you will find the elusive piece that will enable you to retire. The uncertainty of what lay ahead kept the adrenalin flowing as he drove through the sun kissed countryside.

At about one o'clock he stopped at an old seventeenth century country pub with the unusual name of the Hare and Rabbit, which was where his fortunate encounter with lady luck was about to take place.

Except for the Bantam, the pub was empty and as the landlord slowly poured a glass of shandy he bemoaned to Brian that it was hardly worth opening the doors of the pub as business was so bad.

The landlord was a middle aged jovial man, with thinning hair and a pair of grey eyes that looked directly at you when their owner was talking.

He smiled pleasantly at the Bantam as he handed him his change, and returned to the end of the bar, to continue replacing bottles on the shelves from out of a large wooden crate.

Brian took a sip of his drink and gazed idly round the bar taking in the worn furniture, grimy walls and nicotine stained ceiling. A profusion of brass ornaments and a variety of pictures covered the walls in a haphazard fashion, as if they had been placed there without any thought.

His gaze stopped. He picked up his drink and walked casually across the room. A tingle ran down his spine as he looked towards the bar to see where the landlord was. He was still at the far end of the bar engrossed in his bottling up, completely oblivious to anything else. The Bantam walked over to where a grimy picture hung on the wall between two tarnished wall plaques His heart beat a little faster in anticipation.

He peered closely at the picture, the grime covering its surface made it difficult to tell exactly what it was. Set in a Victorian gilt frame, and measuring approximately twelve inches by twenty four inches. The picture depicted a group of people in Victorian dress, in a large field, haymaking. A burly looking man stood on top of the hay cart, a pitchfork in his hands, whilst below him two dogs ran about barking at two small children. A herd of cows were grazing in a far field, and the sun was shining brightly. It really was a lovely painting. And it was an oil. Painted on canvas. The Bantam couldn't see any signature on the picture but knowing a little about paintings, he knew that a painting of that quality would be bound to have one somewhere.

He returned to the bar and started to engage the landlord in conversation. He told the Bantam that he had owned the Hare and Rabbit for about ten years, and that after the recent death of his wife, he was selling up and moving out to live in Australia with his sister.

The Bantam had spent some time living in Australia himself, so he quickly steered the conversation to its virtues and way of life.

Half an hour and a few drinks later, they were chatting happily together as if they had known each other for years, and the Bantam decided it was time to make his move.

'What are you going to do with all the stuff in the pub?' he casually asked, keeping his fingers crossed as he took a sip of his drink.

'Oh, sell it, I suppose,' the landlord replied quietly. 'It's not worth much, but every little bit will help to get me started in Australia.'

'I wouldn't mind a couple of the brass plaques.' Brian smiled at him, and walked over to the wall where the oil painting hung tantalizingly between the plaques.

'I'll give you fifteen quid for them.'

The landlord's eyes lit up as the Bantam pulled out his wallet, and he eagerly held out his hand as he agreed to sell Brian the plaques.

'I'll give you a tenner for the picture as well, if you want,' Brian said in an off hand tone, giving the impression that he was really only doing it as a favour. The landlord quickly agreed, and Brian heaved a sigh of relief.

The Victorian painting was his.

He took the painting and the plaques carefully off the wall, leaving large white marks where they had hung. Calling out a cheery goodbye to the landlord, he gleefully walked out of the pub holding the painting carefully under his arm, an expression of complete nonchalance on his face, his heart pounding nineteen to the dozen with the knowledge of what he had just acquired.

Half a mile down the road, he opened the car window and threw the brass plaques into a ditch. They were worthless, but had served their purpose. But the painting. Now that was a different thing altogether.

When it had been restored and cleaned it would be worth a lot of money, but he wasn't going to sell it. He knew that it would look magnificent over the fireplace in the lounge of Weighbridge House and he couldn't wait to get home to hang it there.

By six o'clock that evening he had covered two hundred miles and had bought quite a tidy load of furniture, which was securely tied to the roof of the Volvo. He felt very satisfied so far with his trip, but when he thought of the painting he glowed with satisfaction.

It used to amaze the Bantam that he was never stopped by the police for carrying such a lot of furniture on the top of the car. Sometimes it was stacked three layers high. But it was a long time before he found out that the police would only pull him in for an insecure load, not for stacking it high on the roof rack.

An hour later he pulled into the car park of the Miners Arms, a small pub that he always stayed in on his trip south. It was situated down a narrow side street about a hundred yards from the sea, with a magnificent sea view from the window.

It was nothing special, in fact if anything, it was a little shabby. But its four bedrooms were always clean, and he was always made to feel very welcome whenever he called.

'Hey Bantam,' a voice yelled across the bar at him as he pushed open the door and walked into the warm bar.

'What are you having?'

The Bantam looked across the smoke filled room to the direction of the yell.

Patrick Flaherty, an Irishman who owned the pub, and ran it with a rod of iron, grabbed his hand and pumped it up and down, a big smile on his face.

Brian was immediately filled with a feeling of well being, and being wanted.

Paddy had this effect on people, and in the five years that Brian had known him, he had never heard him raise his voice in anger, to anybody.

He was plump and jovial, and his completely bald head made him look a little older than his forty years.

'A bath first, Pat?' the Bantam grinned as he took Pat's outstretched hand. 'Then we will see if your food is up to its usual high standard. After which, you and I will see who can consume the most of your most excellent bitter.'

Paddy handed the Bantam a key from behind the bar.

'T bone steak, as usual I presume Brian. I have given you number four. All right?'

An hour later found Brian happily on a stool by the bar, a beautifully cooked T bone steak inside him, and a pint of Paddy's best bitter in front of him. He felt well contented. Pat's wife was an excellent cook, and Brian always thought that if she were given an old boot to cook she could make it palatable.

As he thought about the painting, which for safety, he had brought out of the Volvo and put in his bedroom wardrobe, he absently watched the bar filling up with students from the nearby university.

'A bottle of paint cleaner will soon get all the dirt and nicotine off the painting,' he thought, taking a long swallow of his drink, and a coat of picture varnish will brighten it up. Suddenly he felt a finger running down his spine, sending such a shiver through his body that he nearly choked on his drink. He knew that touch. He knew who loved playing that trick.

Rose!

He turned slowly round on his stool and gazed into the sea green laughing eyes of his ex lover. He felt the old familiar feeling for her return, as he unashamedly ran his eyes over her beautiful body.

'Hello Bantam, my love.' Her soft husky voice sent his pulse racing, as she put her arms around his shoulder and pressed provocatively against him.

'I've missed you. It's been a long time. Where have you been hiding yourself?' she murmured kissing him on the cheek.

Brian didn't tell her that he actually had been down since they had last met, as he hadn't wanted to get involved again. But as her heady perfume wafted over him, he thought to himself that maybe he had been wrong.

The Bantam thought that she was a very desirable woman indeed, and as he kissed her gently and asked her what she was going to have to drink a feeling stirred in his loins.

Brian and Rose spent the next couple of hours pleasantly reminiscing, and it was only when he happened to look at his watch, that they realised how long they had been chatting.

'How do you fancy a Chinese?' he asked 'I feel a bit peckish.'

'I'd rather have a Welsh antique dealer,' Rose replied running her tongue slowly over her moist lips, 'but a Chinese will do for now.'

Once again a tingle ran up the Bantam's spine, as Rose placed a well manicured hand on his shoulder and slid gracefully off the bar stool.

He held her jacket out for her, and as she casually shrugged it on, she slowly turned and looked straight into the Bantam's eyes.

'So how much is the painting that you were telling me about?'

Brian cursed the fact that he had told Rose about the painting. He should have kept his mouth shut.

'Rose, darling,' he smiled fondly at her and kissed her hand. 'I love you dearly, but I'm afraid the painting is not for sale. I told you, I'm going to keep it for myself.'

He groaned inwardly. He knew exactly what Rose was up to. Even though she hadn't seen the painting, she wanted it.

Once they were outside the Miners Arms, Rose tucked her arm into his, giving him a quick peck on the cheek, her perfume making his loins stir once again with unrest.

'How much did you say it cost you?'

The Bantam mentally cursed again. Rose did this every time he bought anything nice that she took a fancy to. Whatever it was Rose had to have it. And have it cheap. Her personal favours were thrown in as bait.

That was why he had finished the affair with her. She was unable (or unwilling) to separate business from pleasure.

Being a soft touch had cost him a great deal of money over the years, but this time he was determined that Rose would not have her way.

'It's a lovely warm night, Bantam.'

Rose squeezed his arm, and snuggled up to him.

'Why don't we take our meal onto the beach. It's far too hot to eat indoors. We can get a bottle of wine to go with it as well. What do you think? Her warm smile would have melted an iceberg.

Brian readily agreed. She was right. It was a beautiful warm night. So fifteen minutes later found them sitting on a low breakwater on the beach, paddling their feet in the ocean and enjoying a Chinese takeaway, two open bottles of wine standing up in the sand beside them.

'This is great darling, isn't it?' she murmured, and held up her glass, which had been borrowed from the restaurant, for him to refill. She put her glass up to the Bantam's.

'Here's to us.' She smiled her sexy smile, with her green eyes full of promise.

'Here's to the sexiest antique dealer that I know,' replied Brian, giving her a big hug, that developed into a passionate kiss.

'Let's go for a walk along the beach,' Rose suggested, wiping her lovely mouth with a serviette. 'Better still, we can go back to the pub and finish the wine off in your room, can't we?'

The Bantam, feeling the effects of the evening, willingly agreed to her suggestion. He felt that he was losing control of the situation, but he was still determined not to sell the painting in spite of all Rose's efforts to seduce him.

Rose broke into his thoughts.

'You can show me the painting. It sounds lovely. I only want to look at it.' She laughed as he went to open his mouth in reply, and planted a warm affectionate kiss on it which did nothing to help his willpower.

They made their way back to the pub, where the bar was nearly empty, it by now being well past closing time.

The Bantam bought a bottle of vodka from Patrick who was busily cleaning up behind the bar. He gave him a broad wink as he passed the bottle over to him.

'Have a good night,' he murmured quietly.

Brian, Rose still clinging to his arm, made his way unsteadily up to room number four, which was on the second floor. He was still determined that Rose would not get the painting. An hour or so later, they had drunk a lot of the vodka, and were thoroughly enjoying themselves with careless abandon, when Rose, rolling on top of him, and nearly falling out of bed in the process, broke the mood.

'Well now my lovely,' she whispered, kissing him lightly on the nose, 'let's have a look at this wonderful painting of yours.'

Brian groaned out loud, and slapped Rose playfully on the bottom.

'You are a bloody nuisance,' he said, as he reluctantly climbed out of bed and walked across the room to the wardrobe, where he had put the painting.

Rose held the painting at arms length. 'It's beautiful,' she said gazing at it in admiration. 'It really is beautiful,' she went on. 'You are right, it only needs a good clean and it will be as good as new. What a fabulous subject.'

She turned slowly towards the Bantam, her green eyes gazing into his.

'Sell it to me Bantam, please. I will give you whatever you want.'

'You have already done that darling,' Brian laughed at her, and taking the painting, he placed it on a chair.

'Please Bantam. Please.' She pleaded. 'Sell it to me. I'll give you three hundred pounds for it.'

'No way, love,' he replied. He was tempted though, oh how he was tempted. Three hundred pounds was a lot of money. But he was determined that Rose was not going to get her way again.

'I've told you Rose.' He put his hands on her naked shoulders and kissed her gently on her forehead. 'I'm going to hang it over the fireplace at Weighbridge House. On that I'm determined and nothing you can say or do will make me change my mind.'

'Three hundred and fifty,' Rose gazed unashamedly into his eyes.

'No, Rose. I have told you, it's not for sale. I mean it. It's not for sale.'

For the rest of that night Rose tried in vain to get the painting. She tried every trick in the book, and she knew a few!

But the Bantam wouldn't give in, and the next morning as he said goodbye to Rose, and to the Miners Arms, it was a very tired Welsh antique dealer who headed wearily home.

But he still had the painting. And the Bantam would always remember the vision of Rose standing in front of the oil painting, stark naked, with a large glass of vodka in her hands, trying in vain to buy it from him.

Chapter Fourteen

Miranda's Piano

As the Bantam drove through the sun splashed countryside, he once again thought of Rose, and the pleasant night that they had shared together. His head ached a little, which was very understandable when you consider that he and Rose had finished a bottle of vodka, on top of all the other drinks that they had drunk earlier in the evening.

The painting was safely wrapped in a blanket in the back of the Volvo and Brian grinned to himself.

'Rose didn't get the painting after all,' he thought, mentally rubbing his hands together with glee. 'But I must admit, it was a very near thing.'

He stopped at a couple of antique shops on the way home, but without much success, and as the day progressed, he was beginning to despair of finding anything else.

The weather didn't help his mood much either. What had started out to be a beautiful sunny day was rapidly turning into a miserable one. Black clouds began to gather and a fine drizzle began to fall.

'Still,' he mused to himself as he turned on the windscreen wipers, 'if I don't get anything else, the painting has made the trip worthwhile on its own. Not to mention the night with Rose!' and he grinned broadly.

At about four o'clock in the afternoon, he drove into the sleepy country town of Pemberton. The rain was lashing down by this time, and for safety's sake, Brian turned on his headlights as it was getting so dark.

'What's happened to summer?' he thought dismally, as he climbed out of the car and almost had the door wrenched from his grasp by the wind that had started to howl down the sodden streets.

He ran across the road into a nearby second hand shop, and after about ten minutes was pleasantly surprised to find that he was able to buy a couple of small marble mantle clocks at a reasonable price.

A few minutes later he drove into the large car park of another second hand shop. It was his last call before he got home, and he was certainly glad that it was because he was tired, miserable and generally fed up, and the outlandish weather didn't help any.

As he got out of the car he felt a strange sensation come over him, as if he was being watched by a pair of unseen eyes. Maybe the feeling was because the shop was actually a large chapel that had fallen into disuse due to the lack of parishioners.

The feeling persisted as Brian, wiping the rain from his face with a grubby handkerchief, pushed open the old oak chapel door, and entered the high vaulted interior.

The feeling became stronger.

At the far end of the chapel were three large stained glass windows, around the walls, memorial tablets had been set into the stonework, and thick black old oak beams supported the roof.

'Hello,' he called loudly. 'Anybody around?'

His voice was thrown contemptuously back at him from the high ceiling.

'Hello. Anybody at home?'

The feeling of being watched persisted.

Outside the chilly confines of the chapel, the rain was pouring down and the sky was getting darker.

The only light came from three dusty naked light bulbs that hung from the ceiling, high above the stacks of second hand and antique furniture that was piled precariously in rows running the length of the room.

The Bantam still felt as if he was being watched.

Suddenly a flash of lightening lit up the chapel, throwing everything into sharp relief. To be followed seconds later by the loudest clap of thunder he had ever heard.

The earth moved!

Another flash of lightening lit up the chapel to be followed immediately by an even louder clap of thunder.

Brian felt a chill crawl up his spine, he felt like a butterfly that was about to be pinned to a specimen board, naked and exposed, but to what he did not know.

But he felt afraid.

'Hi there.'

The Bantam jumped and swung quickly round at the voice that came from behind him. A young, pretty, fresh faced young woman stood before him, a battered kettle clutched in her hand, and a cheerful smile on her face.

'I'm sorry if I startled you.' Her cheeky smile lit up her face. 'I just nipped next door to get some water. Ours is turned off for some reason. Anything I can help you with? Or are you just browsing?'

'Oh you're in the trade are you?' she prattled gaily on as she looked through the window and noticed the Bantam's Volvo estate, with its telltale dealer's rack on the top. 'Would you like a cup of tea?' and without waiting for an answer put tea bags into two large mugs. 'Don't take any notice of the prices,' she went on as she poured the milk into the mugs. 'We are always ready to do a deal. There's none of that ten percent off rubbish with us.'

His heart warmed towards her. It was good to find a real dealer who was prepared to bargain a little, and get a small profit and a quick return instead of holding out for a big profit.

But the Bantam still felt the uncanny feeling that he was being watched.

'Thanks,' he said absently as she passed him a mug of hot

steaming tea. He was gazing around the piles of furniture that filled the chapel.

'I'm called The Bantam. What's your name?'

'Natalie,' the young woman replied picking up her own mug of tea, 'Natalie Cole. The Bantam is an odd name isn't it? How did they start to call you that?'

'It's a long story luv,' the Bantam grinned at her, as sipping his warming tea, he started to wander down the aisles of furniture.

Most of the furniture was not suitable for him. The three piece suites, dining tables and the like were far too modern but with so much furniture around he thought he should be able to buy something with a profit in it.

Sure enough he found a nice little gypsy table, which was in quite good condition, and a little further down the same aisle, he came across a lovely little pine travelling chest. He put them both together so he could work a deal out with Natalie later.

The rain was still pouring down onto the roof of the chapel, and the wind was still moaning around the high bell tower. Once more a shiver ran down the Bantam's back.

Suddenly the sensation of being watched went, to be replaced by a soft warm comforting glow deep inside.

The rain ceased its relentless pounding, and a ray of sunshine stole from behind a cloud, sending its rays through the stained glass window.

Then he saw it.

A Victorian upright walnut piano. The front of it was inlaid with marquetry and a pair of brass candelabra were fixed on either side of the music stand. It really was a beautiful piece of furniture as it stood proudly in the sunlight.

The Bantam stopped in his tracks. He was completely unaware that he had spilt his tea, as he hesitantly walked towards the piano. He slowly lifted the lid, as if he expected something to jump out from inside. Would it be there? It had to be there. On the last white key of the keyboard.

Yes it was! As he looked at the burn mark that he had put there a couple of years before. His heart turned over.

It was Miranda's piano.

'Miranda.'

The Bantam softly whispered her name as he lightly ran his fingers along the keyboard, remembering the woman that taught him so much about life, and who very nearly ruined it for him.

'Are you all right love? You have gone quite pale. Look what you've done. You've spilt your tea.'

Natalie had quietly walked up to the Bantam's side and stood with her hand resting on his arm, a look of concern on her face.

'Er yes,' the Bantam stammered. 'I'm fine thanks. Sorry about the tea.' And he quickly finished the contents of his mug and handed it back to her.

'How much is the piano?' he asked casually.

'Ten pounds to you love, seeing as how you're in the trade.' Natalie answered over her shoulder as she took his mug back to the kitchen.

If she had said a hundred pounds, the Bantam would still have bought it. It was Miranda's piano, and he had to have it.

Regrettably, Natalie couldn't remember how she had obtained the piano, or where it had originated from. She suspected that she had bought it at an auction. But it was so long ago, that she couldn't be certain.

The Bantam now knew why he had felt as if he was being watched. Everything was explained to him. It was as clear as daylight.

It was Miranda.

And Miranda was a witch!

As he drove away from the chapel, after arranging to return the next day with Alf and a trailer to move the piano, Brian's thoughts were of Miranda. Darling, dangerous, Miranda. And he smiled to himself as he drove slowly back to Weighbridge House.

It had all begun about three years previously. He had had a call to go and see some pine furniture that was in a farm about five miles away. He found the farm easily enough. As he drove through the entrance of the drive, the pair of rusty cast iron gates belied the rundown appearance of what obviously had been a thriving farm.

But now the outbuildings had slates missing from their roofs. Old farm machinery stood idly rusting in the fields. It was overgrown and neglected and had an aura of sadness about it.

Brian turned up his collar against the cold wind that was blowing across the barren fields. He rang the old fashioned doorbell, gazing across the neglected front garden as he did so.

'Yes.'

Brian started at the sound of the voice. The door had been opened soundlessly, and standing in the glow of the hall light, which, shining from behind her appeared to give her a halo, stood a plump woman of medium height, about thirty years old, a thin smile on her face. Her eyes matched her waist length coal black hair, and the Bantam immediately felt a sensation of peace and tranquillity surround him as she slowly looked him up and down.

'You've come to look at the furniture, haven't you?' She spoke in a soft Welsh voice. 'I've been expecting you. Do come in, won't you?'

Her well educated voice was musical, and yet it had an authoritative quality about it that gave him a strange feeling. It was as if they were both in one. A closeness. Like a long friendship.

Yet she was a complete stranger to him. He was meeting her for the first time. He felt out of his depth. Out of control of the situation which seemed to be in her hands. He did not understand what was happening.

'The furniture is upstairs.' She beckoned him upstairs with a wave of her plump hand.

As he followed her into a bedroom, his eyes fell on the loveliest pine bedroom suite that he had ever seen.

It was in its original condition, its smooth surfaces lovingly polished over the hundred and twenty years since the day it was made. It consisted of a large wardrobe, a marble topped washstand with pretty pink tiles at the back, and a dressing table.

'They look as if they have been standing there from the day they were bought,' he grinned at her as he opened the wardrobe door.

'They probably have,' she replied, her deep eyes searching into his. 'This house has been in our family for over two hundred years. Although it's doing its best to fall apart now.'

'Mother and father have both gone now.' And her voice went soft and quiet as if she was remembering happier times. 'The farm is too much for me to handle, and I can't afford to anyway. So I'll probably have to sell everything.' Her voice faltered, and her eyes misted up with unshed tears. She seemed to pull herself together with a little shrug of her shoulders.

'Anyway,' she said brightly, as they descended the oak panelled staircase. 'Let's discuss the furniture over a drink. It's Canadian Club you drink isn't it?'

The Bantam was rooted to the spot.

'How did you know that?' He stared at her in amazement.

'Just a guess,' she laughed mysteriously, 'just a guess.'

She led the way into a large, oak beamed, lounge and motioned for him to sit in a high backed leather wing chair that stood by the side of the inglenook fireplace.

'That was my father's chair.'

He made to get up, but she stopped him with a wave of her hand.

'No. Please, sit down,' she smiled. 'You suit the chair. In fact you suit the room very well.' She handed him a cut glass tumbler, full to the brim with his favourite whiskey.

'Do you like music?'

She sat down on the green leather chesterfield, a glass of sherry in her hand and crossed her long slender legs.

'Er, yes, I do.' Brian took a quick swallow of his drink to hide his embarrassment. 'But I'm not an expert.'

They spent the next few minutes discussing the pine bedroom suite, and eventually settled on a price of fifty pounds, which was much more than it was worth. But the Bantam was completely overwhelmed by her and the bedroom suite was going further from his mind as he sat fascinated by the young lady before him.

As Brian took another swallow of his drink, Miranda, for that turned out to be her name, stood up from the chesterfield and walked across the room to a beautiful Victorian walnut piano that stood against the far wall.

Lifting the highly polished lid, and pulling out the piano stool, she gracefully sat down and ran her fingers over the ivory keys, her hair shining in the soft glow that came from the solitary standard lamp standing in the corner of the room.

The soft melody that she skilfully played, bathed the room in an atmosphere of peace. Nothing outside those four walls existed. It was as if time stood still, and they were the only two people that mattered in the world.

Brian, placing his drink on the low table beside him, slowly stood up from his chair, crossed the room, and sat down on a dining chair that stood beside the piano.

Miranda's hands moved effortlessly across the keys. She looked up and smiled at him, her eyes speaking volumes, and Brian, unthinkingly, placed his cigarette on the end key of the piano as he collected his drink from the coffee table.

The Bantam never did remember what Miranda played that night. He was so enthralled by the whole scenario, that the smouldering cigarette went unnoticed until he realised that it was burning the keys, and he hastily removed it.

He apologise profusely to Miranda, who just silently shook her head, and continued playing a soft haunting melody.

Over the next twelve months, Brian and Miranda saw a lot of each other. It was during this time that he discovered that Miranda was a witch.

It happened one Tuesday morning, about three months after the Bantam had met her. He had decided to go on a buying trip, and wasn't seeing her until the weekend.

She lived about five miles away from him, and on this

particular morning he was heading in the opposite direction to her home.

But a short while later found the Bantam driving into Miranda's yard. On entering her kitchen, he found the breakfast table laid for two, and Miranda, a soft smile on her face, waiting for him.

'You're late darling. I expected you a little earlier.'

Miranda had willed Brian to come to her, by the sheer power of her mind. And he had been quite unaware of it and as he sat down to the meal that she had prepared he felt a strange feeling of apprehension.

It was uncanny.

On another occasion, late one night, after going out for dinner, they stopped the car in an old disused quarry out in the country. It was a dark night, the stars were hidden by the black clouds that promised the rain that was to come. He turned the radio on and the soft music permeated the interior of the warm vehicle.

Suddenly Miranda became very agitated and distressed. She seemed to go into a kind of trance and cried out over and over again.

'You poor thing. You poor thing,' she moaned softly, ignoring Brian totally. 'Why did they do it? Why? Why?'

He was completely taken aback by the turn of events, and did his best to comfort her. Miranda by this time had tears streaming down her cheeks, uncontrollably and Brian felt so helpless and inadequate as he watched her crying out in distress.

Later that evening, after she had calmed down, Miranda explained to the Bantam that when they were in the quarry, she had sensed an evil presence all around her, and had seen a small, blonde haired little girl of about five or six years of age, with her head covered in blood. She didn't know what had happened to the little girl but she knew that it had been something bad.

The next day out of curiosity, Brian made a few local enquiries and discovered that about fifteen years previously, a young girl that fitted the description had been brutally battered to death in the quarry. Miranda being the sort of person that she was had seen the spirit of the little girl.

Miranda would frequently will him to telephone her when he was out on his buying runs. He would be quietly driving along the road, when suddenly he would have the feeling that he must telephone Miranda, and sure enough, she was always waiting for him.

But it worked both ways. Over a period of a few months, Miranda taught Brian how to use the powers, that as she explained to him, everybody has got, but few have the ability to use.

There was no doubt about it, Miranda was certainly a fascinating person.

She also taught the Bantam about people. Why they think and react the way that they do. She taught him to observe, and analyse his surroundings, to be aware of what was going on around him.

But she was also very frightening, and it was with a great deal of reluctance that he decided that he would have to finish the relationship. Events were going too fast. He felt that he was getting himself involved in things that he was a little bit afraid of. The door had been opened for him. But after seeing what was behind it, he came to the conclusion that it would be better closed. But in the years to come he was to think very often of Miranda.

As Brian and Alf unloaded the piano at Weighbridge House, the Bantam lifted the lid and gazed at the keyboard.

He rubbed his fingers over the burn mark.

'Where are you Miranda?' he whispered gently. 'Where are you now?'

On the garden wall, a cat meowed.

It started to rain.

Chapter Fifteen

Danny's Bureau

Miranda's piano sat in the Bantam's warehouse for a long time. Memories of the time spent with her rushed into his mind every time that he saw it and he often wondered what had become of her.

One day, as he and Alf were sorting out the stripping patch, and strengthening the tank, a piano dealer from Scotland arrived in the yard. He was looking for old pianos, and when he saw Miranda's piano standing in the corner of the warehouse, a blanket protecting its shining surface, his eyes lit up.

'How much, Bantam?' he enquired as he raised the lid. 'Shame about the burn mark. Some people are so bloody careless aren't they!' he said as he fingered the cigarette burn on the edge of the keyboard.

Brian squirmed inwardly at the remark, and realised that he had to make a decision. Should he part with Miranda's piano? In the end, practicality prevailed, and it was with mixed emotions that he helped the piano dealer put Miranda's piano into the back of his van, and watched him as he drove out of the yard completely unaware of the turmoil that he had just caused.

A couple of days later, Brian was returning from a buying trip that had turned out to be a complete waste of time and petrol. He hadn't been able to buy anything.

It was a clear, mild night and the stars shone brightly like white fairly lights on a Christmas tree. As he drove slowly along the country road, listening to a rather enjoyable play on the radio, he felt tired. He would be glad to get home. It had been a long day and he had had enough. Rounding a narrow bend in the road, he noticed about half a dozen caravans parked haphazardly in the ploughed field alongside the side of the road. He grinned to himself. 'The knockers,' he thought as he quickly braked and pulled into the side of the road. 'They will camp anywhere.'

Over the years, the Irish knockers have removed many tons of furniture from the houses of the unsuspecting public. The methods they used were many and varied, and it must be said, not always strictly honest. Some of the methods sound quite unbelievable, but it must be remembered that the Irishmen were dealing with simple Welsh country folk, many of whom only spoke Welsh, and found it difficult to speak English.

They did not stand much chance against the fast talking unscrupulous Irishmen. The sight of the large roll of bank notes that the knockers always carried would tempt anybody.

One of the ploys that the Irishmen would use was the film set. It was really very simple. Two smartly dressed Irishmen would drive up to a country farm in a new Volvo estate car, or a brand new pickup truck, and say that they were from a film company in Ireland.

They would say that they were looking for genuine old Welsh furniture, to use in a film that was being made about Wales. On seeing that there was an old piece in the farm, they would offer about five times the value of the piece of furniture, explaining that they must have it, as it was exactly what they were looking for.

Whilst one of the knockers was doing the negotiating, the other would surreptitiously jab a sharpened dart into the piece of furniture and sprinkle a small amount of sawdust on the floor so that it looked as if it was infested with woodworm.

On being assured by the farmer that there was no woodworm in any of his furniture, the 'woodworm' holes would be accidentally discovered. After the two Irishmen had put the fear of

God into the unsuspecting Welshman, telling him that the woodworm would go right through his house, he was only too happy to settle for any amount of money just to have the piece of furniture removed. In fact if the truth be known the Bantam had used the trick himself on his brother-in-law.

He had even seen a piece of furniture taken outside, 'Just to have a look at in the daylight, Sir' and one of the Irishmen had 'accidentally' reversed the van into it to damage it and therefore buy it cheaper.

To the farmer, it was a disaster. But to a dealer who restored antique furniture, it was no big problem to repair the slight damage done by a reversing van.

But although the Irish knockers are ruthless with the general public, they are always the first to help out in a problem, and can be very loyal indeed.

They had scant regard for the law, or for paying any taxes, and when challenged by the local authorities would move quickly on to another site leaving the local council to block the entrance to the site with piles of rocks to make certain that they didn't return.

As the Bantam drove slowly and carefully through the open gate and into the field, his adrenalin began to flow as he saw piles of furniture scattered indiscriminately around the camp. A pad foot peeped from under a canvas sheet, and his headlights picked out a yew wood Windsor chair that had been casually left out in the open.

What would he find tonight? The Bantam rubbed his hands together with anticipation. He loved the excitement of the battle of wits dealing with the nefarious Irishmen. Searching through the untidy piles of furniture, it was small wonder that he was addicted to the job.

At the sound of his car, the door of a large caravan nearby opened, and Danny the Liar stepped out to meet the Bantam.

'To be sure, it's good to see you again Banty.' He grinned broadly as he stretched out his hand in welcome.

'Come away in and have a hot toddy to warm you up.'

Danny looked no different from the last time the Bantam had seen him. His hair was still as greasy. He still looked as if he hadn't washed or shaved for a week, and he smelt just as revolting. Remembering the incident with the dogs in his Volvo, he made sure that the doors were all locked before he followed Danny into his brightly lit, comfortable caravan.

Danny's wife, an attractive woman of about thirty five, with typical laughing Irish eyes, handed him a very large steaming glass of hot toddy. Which he accepted gratefully. After about fifteen minutes chatting, in which Brian consumed another hot toddy, that Danny had pressed upon him, they got down to business.

'Have I got a deal for you Banty,' Danny grinned broadly. 'A nice Georgian mahogany bureau. Cheap. Bring your torch and come outside.'

At the mention of a Georgian mahogany bureau the Bantam's thought flashed back to Bob Anderson and the bureau full of sovereigns, and he smiled at the memory.

'I bet this one's not full of sovereigns,' he murmured quietly as he walked across the field, the soil beginning to harden as the evening frost began to bite.

Brian realised that he didn't have his torch with him. Then he remembered he had lent it to Alf when he had been fixing a hole in the attic roof, and the idiot hadn't returned it.

'It's probably still up in the bloody attic.' He cursed Alf again as he rolled up a couple of newspapers to use as a firebrand.

'How about this then Banty?' Danny stood in front of a pile of furniture that was covered with a torn piece of canvas.

'Olé!' he cried and whipped the canvas away with a matador like flourish.

The bureau was, as Brian admitted to himself, a beautiful bureau. There was no doubt about it, its condition was superb. It looked so out of place standing in the ploughed field, eerily illuminated by the burning brand that he held in his freezing hand. Its patina gleamed in the flames, and he noticed with relief that even its swan necked brass handles were still intact.

'How much?' He lit another firebrand from the dying embers of the first, and walked round the back of the bureau. 'And don't get carried away. It's too bloody cold to stand here arguing.'

The Bantam pulled his collar up against the cold wind that was starting to howl across the open field. He wouldn't have been surprised if they had snow before long.

'Five hundred,' Danny replied quickly. 'And that's cheap.'

'I'll speak for you Sir. Give him four hundred and fifty.' A broad Irish voice cried out from behind the circle of light thrown by the burning newspapers.

'No, give him four Sir. You will take four, won't you Danny?' another voice cried out insistently from the darkness.

Brian sighed. The one thing that he feared had happened. One Irish knocker bartering with you was one thing. But when they all started, it was impossible to think straight. Fixing a price in your mind that you were prepared to go up to, with so many people talking out loud together, all perspective was lost.

Which was, of course, the object of the exercise.

The Bantam shivered as he stood in the open field surrounded by excited jabbering Irishmen. His thin jacket was no match for this biting wind, and he was beginning to wish that he hadn't stopped the car.

Danny was in a thin, short sleeved shirt, seemingly oblivious to the elements. Brian knew that Danny the Liar would not have paid much for the bureau, as he had found the telltale 'woodworm' holes in the side of it. He chuckled when he saw them, as mahogany is too hard for woodworm anyway! So they would be hard put to make their home in it.

'Three hundred, Danny.' Brian blew into his cupped hands in a vain attempt to keep them warm.

'Give me a break Danny. We do a lot of deals together, and it's bloody cold.'

'Give him three hundred and fifty,' a voice spoke up again from the darkness.

Eventually they settled at three hundred and twenty pounds, and at that, the Bantam was satisfied.

The bureau really was in pristine condition. It would need no work at all, except for a polish. This was indeed a rare event when buying furniture from the Irishmen, as usually everything needed repairing.

As Brian loaded the bureau onto the rack of the Volvo and continued his interrupted journey back to Weighbridge House, he felt very pleased with himself. He was glad that he had been able to make a career out of his interest in antiques. And thankful that fate had pointed him in the right direction.

The only thing that held disappointment for him was having to return to an empty house. Although it had been quite a while since Alice had left. He still couldn't get used to the loneliness. It was, therefore, in quite a sober frame of mind that he eventually turned into the yard at Weighbridge House.

Chapter Sixteen

Alf and His clocks

It was John Evans who started to give the Irish knockers nicknames. Danny the Liar, and George the First, to name but two. But they didn't object. They took it all in good part. Ironically, the names have stuck to this day.

Including 'The Lord'.

That was the nickname that John gave to Brian, and it stuck with him. The Bantam didn't know exactly why John called him The Lord, but he didn't object. Maybe it was a back handed compliment.

Until providence played a card.

In the drawer of a dresser that he had just got from a house clearance, Brian had found half a dozen plain white moulded plastic copies of a coat of arms, with crossed swords on a shield background. Where they had come from and for what purpose they were made, he had no idea.

He took them to a friend of his and had them painted. After which he nailed them to the doors of the showrooms and workshops around the yard. He grinned as he stood back to admire his handiwork. The shields looked very impressive. Now he felt like a lord. If John wanted to call him a lord he might as well look like one.

One sunny morning a few days later, he was crossing the yard carrying a pine chest of drawers that Alf had just stripped. He was dressed in his old, decidedly tatty, clothes as he had been helping Alf. He certainly didn't look anything like a lord. A loud voice with a Texan drawl hailed him. He knew, without turning round what he would see.

Sure enough, as he swung round, he saw a tall white haired American gentleman standing before him. He was dressed in the usual American style of check pants, jacket, with a pair of white sneakers on his feet. On his head was a large Stetson, that looked quite incongruous in the Bantam's yard.

'Excuse me son,' he drawled.

'I'm looking for Lord Bantam. Can you help?'

Brian never forgot the expression on the American's face as he enthusiastically shook his hand, and asked in awe. 'Are you a real live lord?'

It was all a lot of fun, but eventually it became an embarrassment.

Brian was in the habit of going to the local live entertainment theatre in town every Saturday night. It had two bars, a dance floor, and the food was first class.

He had a regular table in the corner of the room, to the right of the stage. He always took his current girlfriend there if he could. Derek Edwards, who managed the theatre, happened to be a friend of his and had heard about his nickname. So, being the good showman that he was, he exploited it to its full advantage. At the end of introducing each act, he would turn to the audience and say, 'Ladies and Gentlemen. We are privileged to have with us tonight, Lord Bantam.; And at the end of the act, (on Derek's instructions) the artistes would turn and bow to the Bantam's table.

This always impressed any American dealers that Brian had taken out for the evening's entertainment. And any young lady that Brian was with would be thrilled to bits.

After a while, though, all the bowing became discomforting to him, and he asked Derek to tone it down a little. This he dutifully did.

Which was about the time that Alf became involved with the LORD.

Brian had never realised that deep down, Alf was quite a religious person and he only found out when the incident of the hat cropped up.

It was in the middle of winter. Cold, wet and thoroughly miserable. They hadn't seen the sun for, what seemed to be, weeks. Alf had been complaining about the bitterly cold weather, and Brian had suggested that he got some type of hat.

'Did you know,' he informed Alf, with a lofty air. 'You lose a third of your body heat through the top of your head. Get yourself a cap Alf, you'll notice the difference in no time.'

Alf, in his usual fashion, slowly scratched his head. 'Aye,' he murmured quietly. So quietly in fact, that Brian barely heard him. 'No doubt the Lord will provide one for me.' On that he returned to the stripping tank.

Brian, not realising the significance of Alf's words, muttered to himself as he struggled to carry a pile of wall clocks into the warehouse. 'If he thinks I'm going to buy him one, he can think again.'

The next day dawned in much the same manner. Cold, wet, and if anything, even more miserable, with still no sign of the sun.

The Bantam looked out of the workshop window across the yard, and a broad grin split his face. Putting his newspaper down, and finishing his tea in one gulp, he went to greet Alf who was coming through the gate. A bright red woollen cap pulled down over his ears, and a smile on his unshaven face.

'I see you bought one then.' He pointed to Alf's luminous headgear. 'How much did that cost you?'

'The Lord provided.' Alf said excitedly. 'I told you that he would provide a hat for me. And he has, hasn't he?'

A look of puzzlement flew across the Bantam's face.

'Explain Alf. What do you mean? The Lord provided you with a hat.'

Alf was only too pleased to tell him. Earlier that morning as he had been walking down the road to work. He had noticed something red lying under a hawthorn bush at the side of the road. On closer inspection, it turned out to be the bright red woollen cap, which Alf quickly donned, and continued on his way, convinced that the Lord had indeed provided him with headgear to protect him from the winter elements.

Brian, trying hard not to laugh, returned to the warmth of the workshop, marvelling at the coincidences that happen in this life.

That afternoon, the bright red cap still pulled snugly around his ears, Alf came to see him, with an unhappy look on his mournful face.

Brian looked up from the wall clock that he was busy renovating.

'What's up, Alf old son? Has the Lord sent you a bill for your cap?'

The remark went right over Alf's head, and he started to recount his tale of woe.

Financial pressures were starting to get him down. He hadn't got much money, and with Christmas fast approaching, and a mounting pile of bills to pay, he was getting quite desperate. Would Brian lend him some cash?

Brian listened to Alf quietly, without comment, until he had finished his moaning. Brian knew that he wasn't going to lend Alf any money. That was for certain. He knew that trying to get Alf to pay back a loan was like trying to get blood out of a stone. But at the same time, he wanted to help Alf if he could.

Then he had a brilliant idea!

'I'm not going to lend you any money Alf.' Brian turned to face him, a beaming smile on his face. Alf looked crestfallen. He had been relying on Brian's help.

'Do you trust me?' Alf nodded silently at the Bantam, a look of complete bewilderment on his face. 'Alf, my friend,' he laughed as he slapped Alf's shoulder, 'I am going to show you how to make money and solve your financial worries into the bargain.'

Alf's face lit up, like a child who has just been promised an ice cream.

'Have you got any money at all?' the Bantam asked.

Alf nodded. 'About eighty quid, Guv.'

'Right then, come here a sec, let me show you something.' And he led Alf across the workshop to a bench that had a stack of wall clocks lying on it that Brian had just finished restoring.

There were two 'drop box' wall clocks. These had been mass produced in the late eighteen hundreds and were regularly found in chapels and schools. The dial was made up of a thin sheet of tin, painted white, with large roman numerals painted on it, and thin metal hands.

The satinwood or mahogany case usually had an inlay of boxwood and bog oak, and a pair of carved 'ears' were put on either side of the oblong box underneath. This housed the small brass pendulum.

Next to the drop box clocks lay a beautiful example of an American wall clock. About twelve inches wide and twenty four inches long. It was mahogany veneered on a pine carcase. Its glass door had a mahogany strip running across the middle of it. This divided the clear glass at the top from a typical American scene painted on the glass at the bottom. In this case, it was a cowboy roping a steer on the American plains.

The cheap movement was driven by two sugar loaf shaped weights that hung inside the clock on either side. Attached to the back of it was the maker's label, still in perfect condition.

Another favourite wall clock of Brian's was lying on top of the pile. He lovingly picked it up and looked at it.

It was a French wall clock made from papier mâché. It had a pretty fluted edge and was inlaid with mother of pearl. This encircled a convex enamelled dial, and the French movement was of good quality.

Brian slowly replaced the French clock back onto the pile and turned to face Alf. Alf's face still held an expression of bewilderment.

'Give me the eighty pounds that you've got, and I will sell you all these clocks.' He held up his hand for silence as Alf was about to reply, a look of bewilderment still on his craggy face.

'I will then tell you where to take them.' He went on, placing his hand on Alf's shoulder. 'And I will tell you how much to ask for them. I guarantee that you will make forty pounds profit on them.'

Alf looked totally bemused. He gazed blankly round the workshop as if trying to get some inspiration from the tools that were hanging on the walls.

'You do trust me, don't you Alf?'

Alf removed his cap and scratched his head. He was getting out of his depth. But he needed some money desperately.

'Forty pounds profit you say. Straight up?'

As the Bantam nodded, Alf came to a decision.

'All right. I'll do it,' he said slowly, still not quite certain whether or not he had made the right decision. But as the idea grew on him, a slow smile crept over his face.

So the next day Brian concluded the transaction with Alf and duly received his eighty pounds in return for the clocks.

Brian came to the conclusion that he must be going soft. He could have had the profit for himself, instead of letting Alf have it. Still, Alf did need the money and what Brian hadn't had, he wouldn't miss. Perhaps Alf was right and the Lord did provide!

Alf took the clocks round to John Evans, where, as the Bantam had promised, he bought them for a hundred and twenty pounds, giving Alf a clear profit of forty pounds.

'You know the Lord then,' John said to Alf pleasantly, as he stacked the clocks away in his large warehouse.

'Oh yes,' Alf answered reverently. 'I love the Lord. Don't you?' and gazed innocently at John, who turned away quite perplexed.

'Well, I like the Lord, of course,' John replied, assuming that Alf was referring to the Bantam. 'But as for loving him. Now that's a different thing.'

'The Lord is the way, the truth and the light.' Alf grabbed

John's arm and his voice rose in his excitement. 'The Lord provides for us.'

'The Lord has certainly provided for you,' muttered John, as he angrily pushed Alf's grasping hand away.

'You're a bloody head case. Sod off!'

And he stormed out of the warehouse leaving Alf standing nonplussed and wondering what on earth he had said that had upset him so much.

Chapter Seventeen

To Catch a Thief

It was now over three years since Alice had left and Brian had moved into Weighbridge House. Ann was growing up fast and he felt sad that he missed out on all the firsts in her life. Her first day at school. The first time that she rode her bike unaided.

Lately he had become involved with a lady called Heather. She was a little older than him. She had rich auburn hair, blue eyes, a gorgeous figure and a marvellous personality, that on more than one occasion had helped pull him out of the doldrums. Lately he had been sinking into moods of depression. Moods that he was finding increasingly difficult to get out of.

He still hadn't seen his friendly ghost at Weighbridge House, though he often felt her presence and drew comfort form her.

But Heather had seen her!

It happened one cold frosty evening. Outside the freezing mist was swirling making Heather and Brian grateful for the log fire that filled the darkened lounge with the light from the flickering flames in the old inglenook fireplace.

Brian was sitting in his high backed wing chair, silently contemplating his situation, his customary glass of Canadian Club in his hand and a cigarette slowly smouldering in the cut glass ashtray at his side.

Heather was sitting on the leather chesterfield in front of the fire, creating pictures in the flames. An intimate silence prevailed.

Suddenly she looked up at him, an almost whimper like sound came to her lips.

'What's up love?'

Brian looked across. It was plain to see that something had disturbed her. She continued to look silently at him, her face devoid of colour and her mouth slightly open in a look of surprise.

The Bantam went cold, and he knew.

'You can see her, can't you?' he whispered. He could feel the coldness surround him like a fog.

Heather nodded, her eyes fixed intently on a point over his shoulder.

'Don't worry, Pet.' He held out his hand and Heather grasped it, as if grabbing at a lifeline.

'It's all right. She's a friend. It's an old lady in a long dress, right?' In her frightened state, Heather forced herself to nod in agreement.

Then Brian felt the warmth returning. He knew that the old lady had gone again, and he turned to Heather with a reassuring smile.

'Tell me, Sweetheart.' He squeezed her hand, and gently kissed her forehead. 'What did you see?'

Heather, her voice still trembling, told him that she had seen an old lady standing behind his chair, her arms stretched out as if protecting him, and a sweet smile on her old wrinkled face.

It was then that Brian realised that whatever happened in his life, he would be protected, and he felt comforted by the thought.

The mood was rudely shattered by the shrill ringing of the telephone. Switching on the lamp at his side, he picked up the offending instrument.

The call was from a Mr Evan Davies who lived about eight miles away. He had some antiques to sell, and could the Bantam come straightaway?

Looking over at Heather, he could see that she was still not sure that she had really seen something, or whether it was all in her imagination.

An hour later saw Brian, his hair plastered to his head by the rain that had started to fall and was now coming down in sheets, standing in the untidy lounge of Mr Evan Davies' home.

The son of a Welsh farmer, Evan Davies was a small man with pinched features, his beady eyes constantly in motion. Brian thought that he was in his late thirties, although he could have been a little bit older.

He had a couple of rather nice cast iron Britannia pub tables to sell, and a marvellous stuffed salmon that lay resplendent in a large glass case.

'I don't really want to sell them,' he explained to Brian in a high wheezy voice caused by a lifetime of heavy smoking.

'I don't have any real use for them,' he went on, his eyes closing against the smoke that rose from the stub of the cigarette clamped between his yellowing teeth, the ash threatening to fall to the floor at any moment.

'How much?' Brian asked, secretly admiring the lines of the sleek salmon. He could picture it swimming free in some faraway forgotten river in Wales.

They finally agreed on a price, and at Evan's insistence, they adjourned to the local pub for a drink to clinch the deal.

They talked for an hour or more. Evan told the Bantam that he was very interested in the antique business, and how he would very much like to get involved in it. For his part Brian was only too pleased to find someone who was interested in what he did for a living, so he happily discussed the trade with him.

They parted after Brian had extended a warm welcome to Evan to come to Weighbridge House any time that he wanted to. This Evan did the very next day, and continued to do so at every opportunity. Much to Alf's disgust.

'I don't like 'im,' he grumbled to the Bantam one evening as he was preparing to leave for home. 'His eyes are too close together. I don't trust 'im.'

'Rubbish,' snapped Brian, dismissing Alf's comments with a

wave of his hand. 'There's nothing wrong with him. It's all in your imagination!' and turned to lock the door of the workshop.

One evening about three months after meeting Evan, Brian was returning home from a call, about fifteen miles from Weighbridge House, where he had bought a pine chest of drawers.

He was ecstatic. It was the finest pine chest that he had ever seen. A chest of real quality. It was a perfect size with four small bun feet, a little rail at the back and the original white enamelled knobs on each of its six drawers.

He was delighted with it as he knew that it would strip well, and for the price that he paid for it, would realise a handsome profit.

Heather sat beside him as they excitedly discussed the piece. Heather getting as enthusiastic as he was about it. These days she was getting more and more interested in the business. The Bantam was thrilled with her increasing involvement because he realised that a strong bond was growing between them helping to alleviate his loneliness.

As they drove through the clear moonlit night, back to Weighbridge House, Brian felt strangely content. He decided that they would stop at the next pub and have a drink to celebrate.

This they did, and after about two hours, they continued their homeward journey. Heather snuggling peacefully up to him, her head lying on his shoulder, her eyes half closed in sleep.

Suddenly the peace was shattered by the high wailing of a siren. As the Bantam glanced into the rear view mirror, he could see the revolving blue light of a police car, piercing the darkness of the night behind him.

'Oh no!' he exclaimed in exasperation, as he jammed his foot on the brakes, and pulled over to the kerb, causing Heather to wake in surprise.

'Not the insecure load again,' he said under his breath. Brian had, on many occasions, been pulled in by the police for having an insecure load, and had begun to get used to it. A Volvo piled high with furniture always caused comment. He assumed that this was just one more incident.

But he was wrong.

As he wearily got out of the car and made his way to the police car that had pulled in behind his Volvo, its searching blue light still illuminating the surrounding fields, he cursed silently.

'Damn. This is all I need.'

'Do you know that your lights are not on Sir?' the young fresh faced policeman climbed out from behind the wheel of the patrol car and walked slowly towards him. Taking his notebook out of his pocket as he did so

Brian whirled round in surprise to look at the Volvo.

The policeman was right. The Volvo sat smugly by the side of the road, without a light to be seen. Brian cursed his carelessness.

He had forgotten to turn the lights on!

How stupid can he be?

'Can I see your driving licence please Sir?'

He turned to face the policeman, apologies forming on his lips, only to die quickly as he saw the young constable extract a breathalyser kit from the rear of his car.

Now he was in a lot of trouble.

A few weeks later the court gave him their verdict. He was to be deprived of his driving licence for twelve months and fined a hundred pounds.

He was shattered.

Heather was demented.

Evan smiled!

'Now don't you worry Bantam bach,' he said cheerfully. 'I can drive you round. My back is playing hell with me and I can't do much these days. You know Alf can't drive, so let me be your driver. I won't charge you much. Things won't be so bad.'

Brian had no choice. His back was up against the wall. If he wanted to remain in the antique trade he had to be mobile. Heather was unable to drive, and in any case she had her own full time job to look after. So, after a great deal of trepidation, he agreed to pay Evan forty pounds a week to be his driver.

Reluctantly, he handed the keys of his beloved Volvo to Evan. Later that night as he watched Evan drive the Volvo away, he felt very uneasy about what he had done. Had he known what the future would bring he would never have done it.

For the next few weeks everything seemed to be going very well. Evan was driving him around and things seemed to be all right. Brian had stripped and waxed the pine chest that Heather and he had been carrying on that fateful night. It looked superb. With its honey coloured surface gleaming with the three coats of wax polish that the Bantam had lovingly applied, it had come up better than he had dreamt it would.

'It's a shame to sell it,' he thought out loud as he replaced the tin of wax on the shelf in the workshop. 'But I must survive. Especially now that I have the added expense of paying for a driver.'

'How much did you pay for it Bantam?' Evan enquired when he saw it. 'You're selling it for fifty pounds. So you must have paid well for it.'

'Fifteen pounds,' Brian replied, not thinking that he was adding another item to the storehouse of knowledge that Evan was slowly building up.

'It should sell for fifty quid to someone in the trade, without any trouble. In fact it should make more.'

Brian was getting very frustrated at not being able to drive, and decided to take up some of the time with another trip to America to see JC. He could probably get him to have another container load of furniture. He also decided to take Heather with him. When he told her, she was over the moon with excitement. Evan had agreed to look after things whilst they were away, and promised to see that Alf behaved himself.

A few days later Evan drove Brian and heather to the airport. Evan was as excited as Heather at the prospect. He had never been to an airport before. And even though he wasn't going to be flying anywhere, he was still like a child with a new toy.

As the cumbersome aircraft lifted off the tarmac and into the clear cloudless sky, the Bantam had a feeling of unease at leaving Evan in charge, and expressed his doubts to Heather.

'Don't worry,' she said, squeezing his arm. 'Everything will be all right.'

Two weeks later, they returned from their successful trip to the States. JC had agreed to have not one, but two containers of furniture. So Brian was well pleased with himself.

Evan met them at the airport in the Volvo. Brian suspected that he had cleaned it especially for the occasion, as even the ashtrays (which were always full to overflowing) had been emptied and washed out.

'Have a good time, did you?' Evan asked, as he deftly negotiated the busy airport traffic.

'Things have gone up, you know,' he went on. 'Pine chests of drawers have gone up to eighteen pounds.'

'Come on Evan, I've only been away for two weeks. They can't have gone up that much,' Brian laughed. 'It's just that you have been paying too much!'

On checking the stock later that evening, Brian was pleasantly surprised to see that quite a lot had been sold, but he was a little concerned that most of it had been sold below the asking price.

He asked Evan about the pine chest of drawers, as he noticed that it too had been sold below the asking price of fifty pounds.

'Oh yes, the pine chest,' Evan answered glibly. 'I sold it for thirty five pounds to the trade. There was no interest in it privately,' he grinned at the Bantam.

It was only then that Brian started to wonder what had been going on whilst he had been away. He went to find Alf, and asked him.

'Don't know, really Guv,' he answered with a vacant look on his face.

'I was off sick for about ten days. I didn't see a lot of him.' He pointed contemptuously to Evan who was on the far side of the yard.

'Bloody Welsh git,' he added forcefully. 'You would think he owned the bloody place, the way he was strutting around all the time, giving his orders.'

The Bantam suspected that Alf went sick for a reason, that reason being that he couldn't stand Evan Davies. But he didn't press the point.

It was about three days after his return that his suspicions were confirmed.

He had a local call to go and see a piano, and as it wasn't very far away, he decided to go over that evening to see it. If he bought it, Alf and Evan could go and pick it up the next day with the trailer.

It was about half past seven, and a cold wind was blowing strongly, causing him to pull up his collar against it, as he walked the quarter of a mile or so to the call.

As he rang the doorbell, cursing the wind, which was now beginning to bring with it a few spots of rain, he wondered again about the situation at Weighbridge House, and what had gone on in his absence.

As the front door opened, and he was ushered in by the middle aged lady that stood in the hallway, he ceased to wonder.

He knew.

Standing against the far wall of the lounge, a late nineteenth century carriage clock on top of its shining surface, stood the pine chest of drawers that Evan said he had sold to the trade for thirty five pounds.

'Do you like it?' the lady enquired, as he crossed the room for a closer inspection. 'I bought it at Mr Davies' antique shop for eighty pounds. It was a bit expensive, but I fell in love with it and I had to have it.'

'Do you work for Mr Davies then?' she went on, not suspecting that the Bantam was by this time seething inside at Evan Davies' dirty trick.

Later, when he returned to Weighbridge House, he made a few telephone calls, and everything began to fall into place.

Whilst the Bantam had been in America, Evan had been selling his stock off cheap and replacing it with goods that he had bought himself from the dealers that he had met when he was driving the Bantam around. Evan had said that he was buying for the Bantam, so of course, he had got everything at trade price. He had even had the gall to tell everybody that he and the Bantam were partners.

Brian was livid. As one dealer had said to him, 'You should go away again, Bantam. The stuff has never been so cheap. We all thought you were partners.'

When he saw Evan the next day, he denied it all. He was most indignant that Brian would suspect him of robbing him.

'The keys,' he said coldly to Evan, holding out his hand. 'The keys to the Volvo.' But Evan refused to return them and drove out of the yard.

That night, Brian made his way over to Evan's yard. It was a cloudy night with no moon and he knew that at this late hour Evan would be in bed. Using a spare set of keys, and risking the wrath of the law if he was caught, he drove the Volvo back to Weighbridge House.

It felt strange to be driving again and he was constantly on the lookout for a police car. But this time, fate was kind to him and he managed to get the Volvo back without mishap.

The next day, he told Alf about the incident. Alf was busily engaged in eating yet another Swiss roll. His teeth once again on the ground beside him.

'I told you he was no bloody good. Didn't I? I did tell you.' And he cackled with glee, spraying Brian with a shower of crumbs, much to Brian's disgust.

Chapter Eighteen

It's all in the Wood

Once again the Irish sea was rough.

The Bantam stood on the deck of the ferry leaning against the guard rail, the wind blowing the fine spray into his face.

Overhead, seagulls dipped and dived, their harsh cries filling the air as they searched in vain for food, and the Bantam felt at ease.

He was back on the road again and back at sea. Taking another buying trip to Ireland. As he watched the bow of the ship dip casually into the white capped waves, he recalled the young lady that he had met on his last trip across the Irish sea. He smiled to himself at the memory of the dejected expression on her pretty face as she succumbed to her seasickness.

Brian thought that it was quite a coincidence that it always seemed to be rough when he travelled over to Ireland. He didn't mind though. As far as he was concerned, the rougher it was the better he liked it.

As Holyhead receded into the early morning mist behind him, the familiar thrill of travelling again came over him. He had travelled to over thirty countries so far and it never ceased to excite him. He loved meeting different people, exploring their cultures and beliefs. And of course the food.

'It must be the wanderlust in me,' he thought. 'Or maybe I was a seafaring man in a past life.' And he gave a chuckle. Causing a man standing a few yards away to turn his head in surprise.

He recalled a sea voyage that he had made to Australia about ten years previously. As the ship he was travelling on ploughed its way through a force nine gale in the middle of the Atlantic ocean. He smiled to himself as he remembered a young attractive waitress carrying a tray of drinks, doing a complete somersault when the ship dipped into a deep trough. Her tray of drinks were flung high into the air, and she exposed the full length of her lovely, long, nylon clad, legs to the world. He never forgot the incident.

Although it was still rather early in the morning, he decided to go down to the bar and have a drink. The ship was rolling quite heavily now as it left the protection of the Welsh coast and he had to take special care as he descended the staircase that led from the deck to the bar, two decks below.

As he stood at the bar taking his first appreciative sip of his whiskey, he wondered if he should have brought Heather with him.

'She would have been good company,' he mused, clinging tightly to the bar rail as the ship gave a particularly savage roll. Actually the Bantam was getting very fond of Heather, and he found that he missed her when they were apart. He was still haunted by the ghost of Alice though, and he knew deep down that he was a little frightened of getting into another permanent commitment.

'Gosh, it's rough, isn't it?'

Brian's thoughts were interrupted by a soft voice at his elbow and he turned to find an attractive young lady standing beside him.

'Er, yes, it is, isn't it.' He gathered his thoughts together and had a good look at this companion. He guessed her to be about ten years younger than himself with short fair hair, a beaming smile and the most beautiful pair of eyes that he had ever seen. A little on the plump side, (all the more to cuddle, he thought mischievously) she was slightly shorter than the Bantam. She was very smartly dressed in high black leather boots, and a long leather skirt. He bought her a drink, and soon they were talking to each other like long lost friends.

Her name, she said, was Stella, and Brian found her a very easy person to talk to. She had an air of tranquillity about her that was very relaxing. She told him that she was a secretary to an Estate Agent in New York and was going over to Ireland to see an old aunt that she hadn't seen for a long time.

As they talked the Bantam felt himself wishing that he had more time in which to get to know Stella. But all too soon, the ferry arrived in Dublin and, reluctantly, he had to say goodbye to her.

Driving the Volvo carefully down the steep ramp that led onto the docks, he couldn't get her out of his mind.

'I wonder if I will see her again?' he thought as he switched on the windscreen wipers to clear the rain that was starting to fall quite heavily.

'If it's to be, then it's to be,' he murmured philosophically. 'But I must admit, I would like to see more of her,' and a lecherous grin crossed his face.

As he drove along the now familiar route into Southern Ireland, he consoled himself with the fact that Stella had given him her telephone number before they had parted. So it was quite on the cards that they would see each other again.

The rain was coming down in torrents, making visibility difficult, and forcing the Bantam to drive slowly. There was little traffic on the road, and apart from the inevitable tractor pulling a trailer load of peat, he had the road virtually to himself.

His first call was to Paul O'Brien, as he had run out of Poteen.

Brian laughed out loud at the memory of Alf's face when he had given him a taste of the potent Poteen after his first trip to Ireland. He had filled a glass full of the powerful liquid, and the unsuspecting Alf had swallowed it in one long gulp, thinking it was water.

'Bloody hell,' he had stormed as he choked and spluttered.

'What the hell was that? I've never tasted anything like that before in my life.'

When the Bantam revealed what it as, Alf asked him, the next time he got the chance, would he bring a bottle back for him. This Brian promised to do.

'Wait until I give some of that to the missus.' Alf had chortled. 'That'll give her a surprise.'

Knowing what a violent temper Alf's wife had got, Brian suspected that it would be Alf that would get the surprise when she hit him with something. But he didn't say anything.

As usual Paul O'Brien made the Bantam very welcome, and was only too happy to part with some of his illicit Poteen.

'There you go,' he said cheerfully as he handed Brian a large plastic container full. 'It's a fresh batch that I just finished making yesterday. You've come just at the right time.'

After paying Paul, Brian strolled down to the large shed at the back of the yard, and started laboriously to clamber over the mountain of furniture that lay inside. He managed to buy a nice set of six splat back chairs, and a pretty little Irish dresser that was about three feet wide. He also found a small sycamore topped kitchen table that he proceeded to knock apart in his usual fashion. This never failed to amuse Paul, no matter how many times he watched him do it.

After he had loaded the Volvo, he bade his farewell to Paul and headed deeper into Southern Ireland. Brian had intended to go to Northern Ireland on this trip, but Heather had been horrified at the idea.

'Please,' she had pleaded with him. 'Don't go to Northern Ireland. It's far too dangerous. Promise me that you won't go there.'

Reluctantly, the Bantam had promised, although he really didn't envisage any danger to himself. He believed that when his time on this earth was up, it was up, whether he was in Ireland or Timbuktu. But he respected Heather's feelings and returned to Southern Ireland instead.

It was the middle of the afternoon when he wearily pulled into the sleepy little village of Mandel. The rain had stopped, and the sun was struggling to come out from behind the black clouds that had filled the skies all day.

On his last visit, he had noticed a small antique shop tucked away down a narrow side street. Unfortunately, that time, it had been closed for holidays, so this trip he wanted to see if it was open.

'Now where was it?' Brian scanned the street talking to himself. 'Ah yes, that's it. Next to Nolan's Bar. It's open. Great.'

He pushed open the door of the small musty smelling antique shop and peered into the dim interior. He could hear a bell ringing faintly in the distance alerting the owners that a customer had entered the shop. He looked slowly around the gloomy interior and quickly came to the conclusion that it held no promise for him. He saw a large dome topped pine corner cupboard that reminded him of the one he bought from Selwyn a long time previously, but it was too big and cumbersome for his trip.

As he slowly turned to leave, a movement behind him disclosed a frail old lady with skin like parchment standing in the corner of the shop. A black lace shawl framed her face, and fell around her thin shoulders. Giving him a quick glance, she disappeared behind an old Victorian fire screen that presumably led to a rear room.

'How odd,' the Bantam thought, as he picked up a ruby glass bowl, the price of which confirmed his opinion that he would not be able to make a profit out of anything in the shop.

But he was wrong.

Half hidden behind the screen, he noticed a small chest of drawers. It was not very impressive, being covered with varnish and having lost half of its handles. But small chests of drawers were very saleable, and this one could probably clean up all right.

'Excuse me,' he called out.

'Is anybody there?'

'I sound as if I'm at a séance,' he grinned to himself.

'Hello, anyone at home?'

'Yes. What would you be wanting? No need to shout, I'm not deaf.' The frail old lady reappeared from behind the screen.

'What can I do for you?' she enquired, in a voice so quiet, it was almost a whisper.

'How much is this chest of drawers?' Brian asked as he idly opened the top drawer of the chest.

He quickly closed it again, trying hard not to show his mounting excitement.

'Twenty pounds,' the old lady murmured softly. 'Twenty pounds, and that's cheap. It should be a lot more.'

Brian readily agreed to the price, not even bothering to haggle with her, and after quickly thrusting a twenty pound note into the old lady's hand, he started to pull out the drawers of the chest to load it onto the Volvo. As he had expected, they were very heavy. Puffing and panting, he finally managed to get the heavy chest of drawers into the back of the Volvo, and as he drove away from Mandel, and the little old lady, a broad grin split his face, and he yelled out in excitement. He just couldn't believe his luck.

'I gave her what she asked,' he consoled himself, 'I didn't argue with her. It's not my fault if she can't recognise yew wood.' And he laughed out loud.

He had just bought a yew wood chest of drawers for twenty pounds. Even in its present dilapidated state, it was worth at least three hundred.

Yew is one of the hardest woods found in English furniture and because of the number of knots found in it, it is also one of the most difficult to work with. Hence its rarity and its high value.

Yew wood is also very springy, which is why it was used to make longbows in mediaeval times.

Windsor chairs, (named after the town of the same name in Berkshire) were often made out of yew because of the ability to 'bow' the wood to the shape of the chair.

The lovely reddish colour, the weight, and the grain, make it comparatively easy to recognise, but quite a few people do mistake it for walnut.

Brian well remembered, years before, buying a large round Loo table that was veneered in yew. The circular top was veneered with eighteen wedge shaped pieces of yew and it looked magnificent. He had never seen a table like it since, and probably never would.

Later the next day as the Bantam made his way back to the ferry for his return journey home, he felt very satisfied with his trip.

He sea was as calm as a mill pond, reflecting his mood, and, as he drove slowly into the cavernous interior of the large ferryboat, his thoughts returned to Stella.

'I wonder if we will meet again,' he thought as he carefully locked the Volvo and made his way to the upper deck.

'I certainly hope so.'

Chapter Nineteen

A Glimpse of the Past

Two weeks had passed since the Bantam had returned from his Irish trip and the discovery of the yew wood chest.

He sold the chest to the first dealer that saw it. For the princely sum of three hundred and fifty pounds, and was delighted.

He had tried ringing Stella, but all he got for his trouble was an answering machine.

'Damn and blast the bloody thing,' he ranted, as once more the disembodied voice came down the telephone informing him that Stella was not available.

'What's up Guv?' Alf had enquired as he walked into the workshop. 'Ain't there nobody in?'

'Sod off Alf,' Brian turned angrily to face Alf who was casually scratching his backside. 'Go and strip something. Go and do something useful. Just go and do anything, but keep out of my way.'

'Excuse me for breathing,' Alf muttered as he left the workshop. 'Whose bed did you get out the wrong side of this morning?'

'Alf!' Brian followed him into the yard. 'I'm sorry.' Brian smiled slowly at Alf. 'It's just that I'm having a few problems at the moment, all right?'

'Yeh, it's all right. I understand. We all get problems

sometimes. You want to see the problems me and my missus have. She will drive me to drink and then divorce me for being an alcoholic.' And cackling loudly, he walked back across the yard to the stripping patch.

Truth to tell, Brian was having a few problems. In fact he was having a lot of problems.

The main one being Heather.

The business was diabolical. Admittedly he had had a profitable trip to Ireland, but trade in general was terrible. He was also getting a lot of hassle from Heather who was starting to get rather bossy and argumentative.

She was living with him now at Weighbridge House, and was his wife in everything but name. But Brian was not at all happy. He and Heather were two different kinds of people. No matter how he tried, he couldn't seem to get it together.

He tried. Oh, how he tried. But he felt that Heather and he were drifting slowly apart. And there didn't seem to be anything he could do about it.

Brian felt that it was wrong of him to have snapped at Alf the way he did, and he dejectedly returned to the warmth and comfort of his workshop.

He started at the insistent ringing of the telephone, and a small screw that he had been replacing in a clock fell into the sawdust at his feet. He cursed loudly, and grabbed the offending instrument off the wall.

'Yes!' he answered angrily. 'Who is it?'

'Excuse me, but do you do house clearances?' A soft well spoken voice came over the telephone.

'Er, yes,' Brian replied, pulling himself together and putting all thoughts of Heather out of his mind. 'Yes we do house clearances. How an I help you?'

It appeared that the aunt of the lady on the telephone had recently passed way, and she had the responsibility of clearing the house of its contents, and making it ready for sale.

'I'm afraid there's not much of any value,' she said. 'It's only a flat. I just want it clearing. Can you do it?'

Brian readily agreed. He had found from past experiences that there was always something in a house clearance that he could make a profit on. There was frequently something that the owner didn't recognise or didn't know the value of.

He arranged to go that evening to see the flat, and sort out the arrangements. The address was only a few streets away from Weighbridge House, so he decided that he would forego the luxury of the Volvo, and he would walk to the flat.

It was a clear moonlit night. The full moon shone down throwing a clear brilliance over him as he made his way through the deserted streets. The walk did him good. The cool night air cleared his head of thoughts of Heather and the elusive Stella and brought his mind back to the job in hand.

The flat, he was relieved to find, was on the ground floor, and as he walked from room to room examining the contents, a feeling of melancholy came over him.

The old lady who used to live in the flat, had died at the age of ninety two. As Brian went through the house, opening drawers and cupboards, he reflected on the ways of life and the things that the old lady must have seen in her lifetime. The motor car, television, the development of the aeroplane, the telephone.

She had lived to be ninety two years old. The contents of the flat represented her whole life's achievements, and basically speaking, it was empty.

'Is this what life is all about?' Brian dejectedly thought, his mood of depression returning. 'You live your whole life for what? To get some dealer to come and pick over the bones of your possessions and see what profit he can make from them. Is that the final score? Surely there must be something else.'

The feeling of depression enveloped him like a dark cloud. For the first time in his life, he wished that he was in some other business.

When it came down to it, ninety five percent of the contents of the flat would have to go to the skip. There was nothing of any real value, and the Bantam felt the spectre of the flat's tenant standing over him, as if accusing him of desecrating her home.

He idly opened the drawer of a tallboy that stood against the wall in the tiny back bedroom, and his heart seemed to stand still. In a space between the piles of clothing in the drawer, a face looked up at him – it was Heather!

He could not believe what his eyes were seeing. The drawer was lined with an old newspaper from twenty years previously and staring up at him was an old photograph of Heather! On closer inspection he found it to be an article about a trip that she and a friend of hers had won. A trip to Paris. The trip had gone disastrously wrong, and the newspapers had picked it up and made it headline news.

He was stunned. Slowly he removed the piece of newspaper from the drawer and held it up to the light. It was definitely Heather.

A shiver went down his spine.

It was uncanny. He was having problems with Heather. He was thinking of ending his relationship. Then all of a sudden, there she was, staring up at him from an old newspaper.

Fate had indeed played the Bantam a cruel joke.

He pulled himself together, and folding the newspaper and putting it in his pocket, he returned to the job in hand.

The next morning, Brian and Alf returned to the flat to carry out the job of clearing it. It was a lot of hard work, as most of the contents were worthless and had to be taken to the skip. The Bantam was not enjoying it one little bit. It felt wrong. He wasn't at all happy clearing the flat. The discovery of Heather's photograph had unnerved him. He felt as if it was a bad omen.

Memories of Miranda came flooding back. 'Why?' he thought. 'Why should I discover Heather's picture at this particular time? Why now, when I don't feel right about clearing the flat anyway?'

It took them about two hours to clear most of the items until eventually they came to the last bedroom. As they pulled a large, heavy Victorian oak wardrobe away from the wall, they discovered a small cupboard that had been hidden behind it. Brian opened the door of the cupboard and a large grin crossed his face.

Sitting innocently in the middle of the cupboard was an early Victorian pine travelling trunk.

'What have you found, Boss?' Alf peered over Brian's shoulder. His foul breath making Brian wince with disgust.

'It's an old Victorian travelling trunk, old son,' he exclaimed excitedly. 'An old pine travelling trunk.'

Now it must be explained that Brian had always had a soft spot for old pine travelling trunks. Over the years, people have used them for keeping toys or tools in. But their original purpose was as a travelling trunk, much as a suitcase is today.

As he brushed the dust from it Brian's thoughts started to wander.

Between eighteen thirty and nineteen thirty, over nine million people left the shores of Britain because living conditions were deplorable and disease was rampant.

The new industrial age had brought with it a different class of people. The bosses did not look after their workers as did the Lords of the Manor in rural areas, and they were paid very little and had to work very long hours indeed. Young children would work alongside adults. Until Lord Althorp's Factory Act of 1833 set legal limits to the hours that young people were allowed to work.

Conditions were slow to change. There was a lot of unrest. People started to look abroad to seek their fortune. Thus the need for the travelling trunk arose.

The basic box was strong and stood up to the rough handling. This is why they can still be found in abundance today.

They were large enough to carry a family's personal effects. Household items, like the flat iron, the cast iron kettle, and the stone hot water bottle, would be included as important items that would be needed in the New World.

The lidded compartments inside the trunk would have locks,

enabling valuables to be kept secure. One or two trunks would carry a complete family's meagre possessions.

Families could wait up to ten days for a berth on a sailing ship. Lodgings at four pence a night made it an expensive wait, and conditions were usually dirty and overcrowded and not easy to find. The emigrants were an easy prey for footpads, who knew that they would be carrying their savings with which to start a new life.

A berth on a sailing ship usually meant being herded together between decks. In squalid conditions, travelling steerage for thirty days or more.

The introduction of the steam ship in eighteen fifty five eased the discomfort a little. Reducing travelling times to seven to ten days. Large family bunks, typically father, mother and two children, lined the walls of the windowless decks, providing living space for the average family. Trestle tables used for the dining area, were located between the bunks in the aisles and a large water butt was bolted to the deck.

The pine travelling trunks were lashed to the end of each bunk to prevent them from moving about in the rough seas. Candle lamps hung from the beams, giving a scant light in the stuffy atmosphere. The food provided by the skippers would only be water and a few potatoes, the emigrants would have to provide the rest for themselves.

Scurvy was the cause of many deaths during the long sea voyages, and live animals often accompanied families below decks to provide fresh meat. The people who survived these journeys to America, Canada and Australia, were the pioneers who gave life and perseverance to their adopted country and made them what they are today.

'Hey, Guv, look at this.'

The Bantam's thoughts were rudely brought back to the present by Alf who had been examining the compartments in the trunk.

Inside was a beautiful Victorian scrap book. The pages were frail and had the familiar musty smell that is associated with old books. Exquisite handwritten verses in copper plate writing, dated and signed, covered the pages, along with pages of colourful cut outs of birds, animals and flowers.

There were old Christmas cards, and Valentine cards in the romantic style. It was a marvellous find. The Bantam felt as if he had stepped back in time to the private world of Miss J Harris, to whom, according to the inscription on the flyleaf, the book belonged. It read:

To Miss J Harris
from her sincere friend MA Shaw
Sydney, NSW, Australia
November 18th 1880

The Bantam smiled, and thought to himself 'Treasures don't always have a monetary value.'

And as they loaded the old trunk onto the van, Brian felt the dark cloud of depression lift from his shoulders as if by an unseen hand.

Chapter Twenty

From the Hills of Wales to Los Angeles

JC grasped the Bantam's hand so firmly that it made him wince.

'All right Bantam, don't forget now, I need pine to finish off this container. Get as much as you can in the box, but it must be stripped. Take care now, and telephone me as soon as the box is on the water.' And with a hefty slap on the Bantam's shoulder, he turned and was lost in the crowd that was pushing its way into the departure lounge of the busy airport.

JC had come and gone in his usual whirlwind fashion. He had arrived unexpectedly at Weighbridge House at about eleven o'clock in the evening a week previously.

'Just a whim,' he said. His mandatory cigar clenched between his teeth, as Brian had asked him why the surprise trip.

'I just felt like having a bit of a vacation, so I thought I would come and organise another container,' he grinned broadly.

Brian of course was very pleased to see him, as he and JC got on very well and the business would be very useful. Things having been rather quiet of late. Not only that, he could do with the company as Heather had, after a bitter argument, left Weighbridge House for good and the Bantam was on his own again. His first priority on JC's arrival was to lay in a stock of Coca Cola as he hadn't any at all in the house.

They spent the next few days madly dashing around the

country looking for stripped pine. JC had expressed a desire for lots of pine in this container, but it wasn't too easy to find.

'It's bloody amazing,' Brian thought to himself, as he and JC drove down the road early one morning on a buying run. 'Whenever you want something, you can never find it. I bet if JC had wanted lots of oak furniture we would only have been able to find pine!' and he chuckled to himself.

They were on their way to see a pine dealer called Edward Fairing who had a heated stripping tank. With a bit of luck he would have a load of pine furniture for them.

A heated stripping tank is by far the easiest method of stripping pine. The tank has hot water pipes running across the bottom, which are heated by a wood burning stove and as the caustic heats up the paint drops off the furniture. Brian didn't like a hot tank as he was convinced the clouds of fumes that were given off couldn't have been good for your health.

Edward had made a good living from pine. He had been in the business a long time. Brian liked him, and over the years, they had done a lot of business together. Edward greeted them warmly, and, having been alerted by Brian to the purpose of their visit, had kept some pieces of pine to one side for them.

JC managed to buy about eight pieces, including, in the Bantam's opinion, a horrible large pine settle, that was covered in a Victoria pink primer that was made of pig's blood. It looked revolting, and the Bantam knew from past experience that the only way to remove it was to rub it with wire wool, which was one hell of a job and it was almost impossible to get rid of it all. JC wasn't bothered about it as he said it gave the furniture character.

As they loaded JC's furniture onto the roof rack of the Volvo, Edward discretely passed Brian a twenty pound note, which he acknowledged with a broad wink.

It was a common practice in shipping establishments who hosted dealers from abroad over here to buy furniture, to employ a courier to drive them round the country. The shipper would then send their van around to the dealers to collect the buyer's purchases. It was an accepted thing for the courier to have a tip for the introductions, and it ensured the continued visits. It didn't cost the dealer anything, as he usually raised the price of the goods to cover the tip.

Bertram Evans was the next call, he lived in the rolling hills of Cheshire. Bertram had all the trappings of a successful antique dealer. A large rambling farmhouse, a beautiful wife, and two lovely daughters. Not afraid to take a gamble, he was a hard man to deal with, but the Bantam had a lot of respect for him.

As is quite often the case, a lot of people were very jealous of Bertram's success. But Brian knew that it had taken Bertram years of hard work to get where he was, and he deserved his success. Unfortunately they were unable to buy much, as Bertram didn't have a lot of stripped pine. So after a welcoming cup of coffee, and ten minutes chatting about the state of the trade, JC and the Bantam continued in their search for JC's stock.

As Brian watched JC push his way through the crowd at the airport, a cloud of cigar smoke following dutifully behind him, he reflected how lucky he was to have him as a friend and it was with a feeling of contentment that he climbed into the Volvo and set off back to Weighbridge House.

It was about a week after JC's departure and the Bantam was in the workshop chastising Alf for leaving a piece of furniture in the tank for too long.

'It's not my fault,' Alf moaned, 'you should have told me when to take it out. How was I to know it would fall apart.'

'Jesus, can't you do anything for yourself. Do I have to hold your hand all the time?' Brian raved at him. 'If you ...'

The telephone rang shrilly in the corner of the workshop interrupting him in mid flow, and Alf, thankful for the interruption, took advantage of the situation to return to the stripping patch, away from the Bantam's anger.

The call was from an old lady who lived about twenty miles away. She had an old piece of painted kitchen furniture, and was Brian interested in buying it?

He wasn't very enthusiastic about it as it didn't sound very interesting. The weather was atrocious as it had been raining constantly for two days, and showed no sign of abating. But he needed the stock. So, reluctantly, he climbed behind the wheel of the Volvo and headed up into the mountains.

The piece of furniture in question turned out to be the worst piece of pine that he had ever seen.

But it was different.

Sitting in the corner of the lady's oak beamed kitchen, it was painted a terrible shade of green, and looked to Brian to be Irish in origin. Late Victorian, it was a kitchen cupboard that had a flap at the front that lifted up to make a table. It was a 'one off' and the Bantam had never seen its like before.

But it was still horrible.

He was reluctant to buy it at first, as he didn't think that it would strip very well. But mindful of JC's container, he bought it. As he drove home, the offensive piece of pine securely tied to the roof rack, the rain finally stopped.

'Thank God for that,' he thought. And musing out loud said 'JC my old friend, you said you wanted pine, and pine you will get, but this particular piece will be cheap, of that I can assure you.' As it happened, the kitchen piece stripped all right. Although he still wasn't very keen on it, and it was with a great deal of reluctance that he put it into the container.

About a week later, the telephone rang in the Bantam's study. JC's container had just been collected by the shipping company and he was completing the paperwork for it. Picking up the telephone, he was surprised to hear JC's voice booming down the line.

'Hey Bantam.'

Brian winced and held the telephone away from his ear.

'How's it going?'

JC's voice sounded as if he was in the next room, instead of ten thousand miles away. Brian told him that the container had just left and had started its long journey to America.

Why don't you come over with it?' JC asked, his broad American accent grating in Brian's ear.

'You haven't seen my new shop yet and a vacation will do you a power of good.'

He proceeded to ramble on and on about the new shop he had just acquired, and as he did Brian started to think about what JC had suggested. It was true, he could do with a holiday. Since Heather had left, he was getting rather lonely and fed up, and a change of scenery would probably do him good.

He made a quick decision.

'You're right JC. I do need a break. I will arrange to be at your place when the container arrives.'

The more he thought about it, the more the idea appealed to him. It would be a novelty to close the container in England, and open it up in America!

The Bantam remembered the time he had been in America on his honeymoon with Alice. And he recalled their stopover in Las Vegas when he played the biggest one armed bandit in the world. It cost a dollar to play the machine, which was about five feet wide and six feet high. It had a payout of a hundred thousand dollars. Needless to say, the Bantam didn't win, but a few years later he read in the daily papers of an Englishman who did.

The Horseshoe Casino in Las Vegas had on display a million pounds in bank notes sandwiched between two pieces of Perspex, protected by armed guards.

Another casino that the Bantam remembered, had a brand new Rolls Royce standing beside a one armed bandit. The person who won the most money on the bandit after playing it for five minutes, also won the Rolls Royce! The casino was open for twenty four hours a day, so the amount of money that it took in, must have been fantastic.

Yes a trip to the States would do him a power of good.

JC's new shop turned out to be quite large. Situated in a busy shopping precinct on the main road, it was in a very good position indeed. It held a profusion of English and French antiques, as JC also went to France to buy, as well as to the Bantam's.

As luck would have it, a French shipment had just arrived on the same day Brian did. Brian's container wasn't due for another two days. JC and a crowd of helpers were busy unpacking the French container, and Brian was very interested to see how the furniture had been packed. Every item was carefully wrapped and tied, and even the edges of the furniture were protected by straw filled sausages of brown paper. The packing must have cost a fortune.

Brian's container duly arrived two days later, and after it had been unloaded, Brian browsed around JC's shop. He was pleased to find that, with the exception of a broken mirror, all the furniture had arrived safely, although it was a strange sensation to unpack a container in America that you had packed ten thousand miles away in England.

Edward's pine settle was rubbing shoulders with a mahogany chest that Brian remembered JC buying on a previous trip. The settle was being inspected by a young couple.

'It's lovely, isn't it honey?' the young man enthused. 'It's come all the way from England. Don't you just think it's fantastic.'

Brian turned away from the couple still busy looking at Edward's settle, and came face to face with the horrible pine kitchen piece.

'I must confess,' he thought to himself as he walked over to it. 'It certainly looks better here than it did in the workshop. But I still don't like it.'

A smartly dressed, middle aged lady with white hair clutching a huge crocodile skin handbag was inspecting it closely.

'What do you think of the shop, Bantam?' JC's hand descended onto Brian's shoulder, making him jump.

'Great,' he replied, still observing the white haired lady, who was now appearing to be very interested in the pine kitchen piece.

'How much are you asking for the kitchen piece, JC?' he whispered through the side of his mouth.

JC shuffled in embarrassment. 'Five hundred dollars. But you just remember my shipping costs and expenses.'

Brian grinned at him, and playfully punched him on the shoulder. 'Never mind about that, just watch me. I am going to sell the pine piece for you.' And he walked over to the lady, who by now was lifting up the table to see what it looked like.

'It's lovely, isn't it Madam.'

The lady turned in surprise to face him.

'You're English!'

'Yes,' replied Brian, a winning smile on his face. 'Actually, I am an English antique dealer, and have just come over from England with a container of English and Welsh antiques. Including this kitchen piece.'

'How interesting.' The lady rubbed her hand over the table's smooth waxed surface. 'I think it's lovely.'

'Let me tell you its history,' Brian replied slowly, sitting down on a nearby Georgian dining chair. And he proceeded to tell the American lady the history of the pine kitchen piece.

He told her how it was made in about eighteen ninety by the local carpenter, in a little Welsh village up in the hills, how it was used, and he finished up by describing how it finally ended up in Los Angeles.

All right, maybe he did gild the lily a little. Maybe the carpenter didn't elope with the local squire's daughter. And perhaps the tiny holes in the side of the kitchen piece were not caused by shotgun pellets. But the story sounded good. And the lady bought the pine piece!

Later as Brian loaded it into the back of her spacious Cadillac, she asked him if he wouldn't mind going with her to her house, which was just down the road, to unload it for her.

Brian agreed willingly.

When he returned to the shop JC was over the moon that Brian had sold it for him.

A few days later as Brian was sitting in an aircraft flying at thirty five thousand feet over the Atlantic ocean on his way back to Weighbridge House he thought to himself that the ways of the antique world are very strange. Who would have thought that he would buy a piece of furniture and take it out of a cottage in Wales, restore it, ship it across the Atlantic and then be responsible for selling it in a shop in Los Angeles and actually placing it in its new home over ten thousand miles away from where it originated from! It was a strange world indeed!

Chapter Twenty One

The Chinoiserie Clock

lf wasn't very happy.

'What's up Alf?' Brian said brightly, as Alf slouched into the workshop. A hangdog expression on his unshaven face. His hair sticking out like a hedgehog's prickles.

'You look like the wrath of God, Alf. What the hell have you been up to? Didn't you go to bed last night?'

'I never go to bed Guv. I sleep on the settee with the dog.' Alf replied quietly, looking down at his boots as if he was ashamed to look the Bantam in the face.

'You do what!'

'I sleep on the settee, with the dog Guv. That way I can hear if anybody breaks into the house.

Alf's logic was unbelievable.

It appeared that he was so paranoid about somebody breaking into his home that he and his wife would never go away together. Not even for a day out. On most nights he slept downstairs on the settee with the dog for company, which, plus the fact that he only bathed every other week, explained why he was so malodorous.

'So what's the problem old son? Why aren't you happy this morning?'

'I'm broke,' Alf replied solemnly, slowly pulling the wax out of his left ear with a grimy finger.

'Have you got any more clocks, Guv?' Alf's eyes lit up at the memory of the profit he had made out of the wall clocks that the Bantam had sold to him a few months previously.

'Sorry Alf,' Brian smilingly replied. 'No clocks. In fact,' he went on, 'if the truth be known, I too am broke. Business is terrible. I can't remember when it has been so hard.'

A grin split Alf's face.

'You broke Guv. Go on with you. You're a millionaire. You've got all this.' He waved a hand around the yard. 'You can't be broke.'

Brian was about to explain the basics of business, and profit and loss, but one look at Alf, and he changed his mind.

'What's the point,' he thought to himself, 'he wouldn't understand it. He thinks that the Lord provides.'

He put his hand in his pocket and pulled out his wallet. Reluctantly, he took out a five pound note and gave it to Alf. The Lord had provided for Alf again! Alf's face lit up like a child who had been given a bag of sweets.

'Thanks very much indeed Guvnor.' Alf was impeccably polite as he carefully folded the note and placed it safely into the back of a box of matches.

'Don't put it in there Alf,' Brian reproached him, 'you might throw the box away when you've used all the matches and you will lose it.'

'No, Guv,' Alf replied, now trying to remove the wax from his right ear. 'I wouldn't do that. I wouldn't throw the empty box away.'

'What on earth would you do with it then?'

'I keep 'em in a big cardboard box in the shed,' Alf replied, a grin crossing his face, as he successfully extricated a large piece of wax from his ear.

'What the hell for?' Brian asked mystified. 'And for God's sake stop doing that. It's a disgusting habit.' And he knocked Alf's hand away from his ear.

'You never know when I might need them, see.' Alf spoke

slowly as if he was trying to make a child understand what he was saying.

The Bantam shook his head in despair.

'Get on with the stripping, Alf,' he said in exasperation turning back to the workbench.

As Alf happily strode across the yard, stepping in all the puddles that had been left by the previous night's rain, Brian called out. 'And don't forget, I want the fiver back at the end of the week.'

'Some hope,' he thought, as he returned to the pine chest he had been busy waxing. 'Alf will never remind me about it, and I will no doubt forget, as I usually do.' This was true. He had a memory like a sieve. Over the years this had cost him a lot of money.

He had not been far off the truth either when he told Alf that he was broke. He wasn't totally without funds, but things were getting very tight. Brian needed to get stock without paying through the nose for it.

So he decided to have a day knocking.

The next day saw the Bantam, feeling very optimistic, and very smartly dressed, in a little village about forty miles from Weighbridge House.

It was a beautiful day in mid May. The sky was clear. The birds were singing and Brian felt good to be alive as he knocked on the first door.

The spiel that he used was usually the same at every call.

'Excuse me,' he would politely say to whoever answered his knock. 'I am in the area today buying any old furniture, copper, brass or bric-a-brac.' And he would hand them a business card. 'I will give you the best possible price. And will, of course, pay you in cash.'

Nine times out of ten he would be met with a sharp rebuff. But the tenth call usually turned out to be fruitful. Perseverance was the key to success. And not allowing the refusals to demoralise him.

The Bantam, it must be added, was not over keen on knocking. How the Irish knockers did it every day he couldn't comprehend, but sometimes needs must.

By the middle of the day, his respect for the Irish knockers was growing stronger. He had bought a rather nice copper tinker's kettle for five pounds, and pair of pewter candlesticks for eight. But he had found nothing really exciting.

Then he had a stroke of luck.

Knocking on the door of a modern bungalow, without much hope, (modern houses usually produce modern furniture) an elderly, white haired gentleman came to the door.

'I'm so glad you have come,' he said, smiling, as Brian stated his purpose, and beckoned him into the bungalow. 'My sister has just passed away and we have lots of things to dispose of.'

Brian thought his ship had finally come in.

'We didn't know how to get rid of all the furniture. So it is very fortuitous that you have called,' the old man prattled on and as the Bantam stepped into the hallway, he almost cried out aloud in his pleasure. Standing in front of him was a seventeenth century brass dialled grandfather clock, with a narrow oak case, and a deep shining patina. It looked magnificent. Opposite, hanging serenely on the wall, was a mahogany banjo barometer.

He was ushered into a long lounge with French windows leading onto a well kept garden, with a large orchard beyond.

It was an Aladdin's cave!

Against the far wall, alongside the French windows, stood a superb eighteenth century Anglesey oak dresser. In front of which was an oak drop leaf table of the same age, surrounded by a set of six ladder backed chairs.

On the opposite wall hung a double weighted Vienna clock, its plaster horse standing proudly on the top. Beneath this was an early oak blanket chest that had been polished so lovingly over the years, that the sunlight streaming in through the French windows, reflected off it, like moonlight on a still lake.

The Bantam gazed around the room in disbelief. Taking in the mahogany knife box hanging on the wall, alongside the biggest pair of cloisonné dishes he had ever set eyes on.

A pair of genuine Canton vases stood on the mantelpiece, underneath an oil painting that Brian knew for certain could only have been a genuine Stubbs.

He said not a word – he was speechless! So much so he failed to notice the old black vinyl three piece suite sitting dejectedly in the corner of the room.

'The bedrooms are through here,' the old man's voice broke into Brian's dreams, and he obediently followed him slowly out of the room.

A large ugly bedroom suite, that Brian would have been unable to sell, stood by a large battered double bed. On the other side of which was a beautiful little gypsy table.

Another treasure trove was in the large second bedroom. The bedroom suite was late Victorian, with a large mirrored wardrobe, a marble topped washstand, and a triple mirrored dressing table. Next to that was a dark oak bureau with carved lion's head for the handles of the drawers. In the far corner was a matching carved bookcase, but instead of the shelves being filled with books, they were crammed with Rockingham china. Standing beside it, looking quite incongruous, sat a modern rocking chair.

'This,' the Bantam thought as he looked around, still dazed by all he had seen, 'must be the house clearance to end all house clearances. What a find. What a stroke of luck.'

He turned to the old man, a smile on his face, mentally keeping his fingers crossed.

'How much for the lot?' he asked slowly and clearly. 'How much do you want?'

The old man's sudden high pitched laugh took Brian quite by surprise.

'Oh goodness me, no.' The old man laughed again. 'We aren't selling the lot. Well, we are, but not to you.' He smiled benevolently at the Bantam. 'All the antiques are going into auction at Sotherbys,' he went on, quite unaware of the change that had come over Brian's face.

Brian was shattered. All his dreams had been ripped to shreds. The old man only wanted to sell the worn three piece suite, the ugly old bedroom suite, and the modern rocking chair which, on closer inspection, turned out to be broken.

Brian felt like a little boy who had been taken into a sweet shop and then told that he couldn't have anything. He drove away from the bungalow feeling completely deflated.

He stopped the car about half a mile down the road at a pleasant country pub, and bought himself a large scotch.

'Pull yourself together, Brian,' he admonished himself. He downed the drink in one go and returned to the bar for a replacement. 'Oh well, nothing ventured, nothing gained,' he thought to himself. And he resolved that he would carry on with the day's knocking, in spite of the jolt that he had just had at the bungalow.

So for the next few hours, he continued his knocking. But to no avail. He just couldn't come across anything.

Until that is, until he came to the little white walled cottage right at the end of the village.

It was a pretty little country cottage with a small, well kept garden at the front and surrounded by a low, white painted, fence. Hanging baskets were suspended from the rose covered porch. And on either side of the door, a pair of old chimney pots held a profusion of beautiful pink geraniums and dark blue aubrietia.

Brian gingerly knocked on the door, using the old brass lion's head knocker that had been worn smooth through decades of use. The door was opened slowly by a small elderly lady, who must have been in her mid eighties. On hearing his spiel, she invited him in with a smile and ushered him into the small, oak beamed, front parlour of the cottage.

'Come in young man,' and, with a wave of her hand, she indicated a splat backed chair that was placed next to the warm fireplace. 'Sit down and have a cup of tea.' She called out in her soft Welsh voice. 'Mabel! Mabel!'

'Drat the girl,' she muttered to herself, as she raised her voice. 'Mabel, come her. We have a visitor.'

The door opened, and instead of a young woman, which Brian had expected, another old lady, who by her appearance was clearly her sister, came into the room.

'Make a cup of tea Mabel,' the woman said in an authoritative voice. 'This young man has come to see if we have anything to sell. I don't think we have, have we?' She turned to him, and said softly, 'She's my sister you know. She's a little younger than me, but she really is so slow.'

Brian warmed towards her. If her sister was younger than her, it must have been by about half an hour! It was such a pleasant change for him to be welcomed into someone's home, instead of getting all the rebuffs and as he sat comfortably sipping his tea by the warmth of the fire, he explained to the two sisters all about his business. He felt very relaxed and comfortable with them.

They told him that their father used to have a large farm in the area, and when he passed on, everything, after death duties had been paid, had come to the two sisters. Unfortunately, all that was left, was enough to buy the little cottage and give them a small monthly income.

'And the clock of course,' the elder sister said.

'Would you like to see it?' the younger of the sisters enquired as she handed the Bantam another cucumber sandwich. Brian's ear pricked up, like a horse hearing the approaching footsteps of his master.

'Er, yes please. If I may,' he said enthusiastically. He stood up, and carefully placed his empty bone china teacup on the tray.

For the second time that day, the Bantam was dumbfounded!

In the corner of the dining room. Its horns touching the top of the low ceiling, was a George II, green chinoiserie lacquered longcase clock. In as good a condition as if it had been made yesterday. Engraved on the brass arched dial was 'WILLIAM

LAMBERT, LONDON.' It was really a wonderful example of early eighteenth century workmanship.

As the Bantam ran his hands over the smooth lacquered surface, he wondered at the miles that the clock case would have covered in its lifetime. As was the custom at that time, longcase clocks would be sent by sea to China to have the beautiful finish applied to the case of the clock. It was a common practice, if a lengthy one, given the speed of the sailing ships of the day. On some occasions, only the door of the clock case would be sent, to save some expense.

The Chinese were experts at the art of chinoiserie, and it would take many, many months for the case of a longcase clock to be made in England, shipped out to China, lacquered, then returned to the clock maker to be reunited with the movement.

'If only you could talk,' he murmured as he stroked his hand fondly over the smooth surface of the clock. 'What tales you could tell. Of the places you have been, and the people you have seen. The loves and lives that have been acted out beneath your brass face. How many lives have come and gone alongside the steady ticking of your heavy brass pendulum, as time ticks unfeelingly by.'

The Bantam did all he could to persuade the sisters to part with their clock. He even offered them a hundred pounds more than it was worth. But to no avail. The sisters would not sell. It was the last of their old family home, and they would not sell it under any circumstances. Frankly, Brian didn't blame them. It was a lovely lock, and it deserved to stay in the family.

Although, as he admitted to himself as he drove away from the cottage, he would have dearly loved to have owned it.

It was a pleasant end to a long and very frustrating day and as the Bantam drove home through the quiet country lanes, the dusk just starting to throw its dark shadows into the night, he forgot all about the two sisters and the chinoiserie clock.

Until three weeks later.

It was a typical day in June. The sky was blue, and the sun

shone down, giving warmth and comfort to the countryside, as Brian contentedly drove towards John Adams' yard.

He was making his usual trip to John's to see what he could find. John did so much business with the Irish knockers, that it was only common sense to go there regularly, as the knockers were bringing him stuff every day. Two large transit vans, bursting at the seams with antique furniture, were parked in John's large yard.

He also noticed Danny the Liar's van, complete with a large, fully loaded, trailer pulled up against the far wall.

Seeing them there he groaned to himself. He knew that it was going to be a long morning. John had to buy all the knocker's furniture before he would even contemplate selling any of it to the Bantam. It was all going to take time. John had his priorities right.

Danny greeted him with a broad grin, and a hard slap on the shoulder.

'Banty, my old mate,' he said warmly. 'And tell me now, truthfully.' He held his finger to the side of his nose in a gesture of conspiracy. 'Did you make a few bob out of the mahogany bureau that you bought from me?'

Brian remembered the cold night, standing by the light of a burning newspaper, buying the bureau from Danny. And he laughed.

'Yes my friend,' he said warmly, 'I sold it well, thanks to you.'

'I've got some good gear here today for John.' Danny the Liar enthused warmly. 'Just come and look at this clock, Banty.' And he opened the rear door of the transit.

The Bantam froze!

There lying on its side, surrounded by rough pieces of furniture, much like a queen bee surrounded by its workers, lay the two sisters' chinoiserie clock. The Bantam's anger began to rise, and he grabbed Danny's arm.

'Where the hell did you get that from?' he stormed, as Danny looked at him in silent amazement. 'I'll tell you where you got it from,' he raved on, oblivious to Danny's shocked expression. 'You conned it out of two little old ladies. You bastard!'

Brian was so incensed at the thought of the old ladies being tricked out of the clock, that his anger knew no bounds.

'Hey Banty, slow down.' Danny held out his hands in a gesture of defence. 'Don't go on so. Let's talk about this. If it upsets you so much, let's talk about it.'

Brian eventually calmed down and Danny told him the full story. It appeared that Danny had gone knocking with 'George the First', and they had called at the cottage of the two sisters. They had offered a thousand pounds for the chinoiserie clock, (bearing in mind that the actual value was nearer four hundred). As Danny the Liar attracted their attention with the case, George the First removed the hood to check for worm.

He had quickly put the dart in the hood, and gone to the carcase of the clock, and while the sisters weren't looking, cut the catgut that held the weights. Needless to say, the weights had mercilessly crashed down, smashing through the base of the clock, leaving it in pieces. It was all done so smoothly, that the two old ladies didn't realise what was happening.

'We finished up buying it for fifty quid,' Danny bragged to the Bantam, 'but don't tell John that. It's a good job we got the two old biddies to sign a receipt,' he went on, 'because they sent for the police. They came just as we were driving away.' And Danny threw back his head and roared with laughter.

'Silly old buggers.' He laughed again.

Brian could quite happily have strangled Danny. He thought of the two old ladies who had given him tea and cucumber sandwiches only a few weeks previously.

He felt so sad.

Two dear old ladies, nearing the end of their lives. Conned out of their last family possession by Danny the Liar, who felt no more compunction than if he had swotted a fly.

Brian got hold of Danny's collar in silent rage. Then he dropped his hand wearily to his side. It would do no good to get mad with Danny. He knew no better. He had no feelings for his fellow man. It was dog eat dog in his world, and the devil take the hindmost.

Later, as Brian pulled slowly out of John Adams' yard, still seething at the thought of the two old ladies being cheated out of their beautiful clock, his thoughts went back to his ex brother-in-law, Bill.

Brian had conned Bill into selling him a clock for forty pounds, when it was really worth an awful lot more.

So was he so different from Danny the Liar, when all was said and done?

Somehow, it didn't seem the same. But deep down, Brian knew that he had no right to pass judgement on Danny. He, the Bantam, had done the same. If not worse. He had done it to his own family. Which was even more unforgivable than doing it to a stranger.

So it was with a very troubled mind, that he returned to Weighbridge House. And in the years to come every time he passed the two sisters' country cottage he remembered the incident of the Chinoiserie clock.

Chapter Twenty Two

Reflections

Later that night, the Bantam sat in his high wing backed chair in the lounge of Weighbridge House listening to the wind that was howling outside, as if trying to gain access to the quiet sanctuary in which he sat.

Flames from the log fire, nestling in the old inglenook fireplace, reflected in a set of large copper urns that sat on top of the seventeenth century oak dresser against the wall. Darkness had fallen, but the Bantam, a glass of whiskey in his hand, was so deep in thought, that it hadn't occurred to him to turn on the light.

He sat reflecting on the past, in the light of the flickering flames. 'What have I achieved since I came into the business?' he asked out loud, and took another sip of his drink. 'True, I have learnt a lot about the antique trade, and, I must admit, I have learnt a lot about myself. But at what cost? Alice has gone. Heather has gone. There is only Ann left, and I don't see her very often these days as she is growing up quickly into a young lady.'

He stood up from his comfortable chair and crossed the room to refill his glass from the crystal decanter that sat on a silver tray on the oak dresser.

The wind continued to moan down the chimney, and Brian felt suddenly cold.

'Oh,' he chuckled, 'so you're still here are you?' He addressed the unseen ghost of the lady in the brown dress. 'You are the only one that has stayed with me from the beginning. At least you haven't deserted me.' And he held his glass up in a silent toast to his invisible guest.

'Cheers lady in brown.' He laughed, and emptied his glass in one swallow.

'Brian, old lad,' he mused aloud, 'I think you are getting a little drunk. You're talking to someone you can't even see.' And he laughed again.

'But you are here, aren't you?' He raised his voice and looked to the far corner of the room. 'I know you are here, because I can feel you near me. Why don't you let me see you? Go on, let me see you, just once?'

The coldness left him, and he knew that his guest had gone again. 'I'm sorry,' he murmured softly. 'I didn't mean to offend you.' And he returned to his chair.

He sat cursing the wind. If there was one thing that he couldn't stand, it was the wind blowing. He took after John Adams in that respect. As he thought of the wind and John Adams, a grin crossed his face and he remembered.

It was a wet and windy day in March, when Brian decided to make a call on John Adams. The wind was blowing so hard that it threatened to blow him off his feet as he crossed the large tarmacked yard to John's workshop.

'What brings you out on such a day?' John enquired, as he paused in the process of replacing a pair of handles on a late Victorian mahogany chest of drawers.

'This damned wind,' he went on, not waiting for an answer to his question. 'It's just blown the bloody roof off the large shed!'

Brian couldn't help laughing at the expression on John's face.

'It's not funny,' John sand angrily. 'I've just spent a fortune replacing that roof. And before I could get it finished, the wind came and smashed the bloody lot. I'll have to start all over again now,' he moaned.

Brian warmed his hands over the pot bellied stove that stood in the corner of John's small cosy workshop.

'I just thought you might have something new in that I could buy,' he said. 'Something I can make some wages out of.'

'Have a look in the warehouse, old son. I'll be with you as soon as I have finished replacing this handle.'

Brian reluctantly left the comfort of John's workshop, and crossed the yard to the warehouse. He cursed the wind that was now growing even stronger, and turned his collar up against the rain that was beginning to fall.

'Bloody weather,' he thought as he wrenched open the door to John's warehouse, only to have it snatched from his grasp as it crashed against the side of the building.

'Damn.' He grabbed the door, and quickly entered John's warehouse, slamming the door firmly behind him. He found the light switch, and the warehouse was instantly bathed in a soft glow that came from the small spotlights cunningly concealed in the ceiling.

The warehouse was about thirty feet long. Its walls were lined with Welsh dressers, oak court cupboards, grandfather clocks and numerous antiques. The Bantam gave a low whistle.

'John's got a few bob's worth here,' he thought as he slowly walked around the showroom inspecting the various items of furniture. His attention was caught by a beautiful seventeenth century oak Welsh dresser standing in the far corner of the room. A large 'sold' label was tied to the rack.

'At least you have made some profit this week, old son,' he said out loud.

The dresser was in lovely condition. Its patina superb. Apart from a piece broken off the rack, there seemed to be little wrong with it.

'Do you like it?'

Brian spun round in surprise, to find John standing behind him, a smile on his face.

'Er, yes. It's great. Pity about the piece missing off the top of the rack through,' he replied, regaining his composure. 'Why don't you fix it John?' he went on. You're a good cabinet maker. It would be simple enough for you to fix, surely?'

John threw his head back and roared with laughter. 'Fix it Bantam. Fix it.' He grinned at Brian, and put his hand on his shoulder. 'I made it!' and he laughed again at he astonished look on Brian's face.

'You mean, you made the dresser.'

'Yes, Bantam my old friend. I made the complete dresser. The lot. Including the piece missing off the top.'

'Good God,' Brian gasped in surprise. 'I knew you were good John. But I didn't know you were that good. Why did you leave that piece broken on the top?'

'It's very simple, Bantam.' John sat down carefully in a Victorian Windsor chair nearby. 'I made that dresser out of old oak. Leaving the broken piece at the top of the rack gives people something to have a go at. While they are complaining about the broken piece, and trying to get me to reduce the price, they are not looking too hard at the rest of the dresser.' John laughed.

'You crafty old devil.' A grin crossed the Bantam's face. 'And you've sold it as well.'

'Yes. And would you believe it, to an oak dealer. He thought he was getting the deal of a lifetime.' And John laughed again. 'Come on back to the workshop. I'll make you a cup of coffee.'

Ten minutes later, they were sitting comfortably by John's stove, drinking warming cups of coffee, whilst the wind continued to howl outside. It was raining quite heavy now, lashing mercilessly against the workshop window. They sat talking about the trade, and various dealers that they both knew.

'Tell me John,' Brian asked, taking a sip of his coffee and feeling the warmth course through his body, 'whatever happened to Arthur Mallory?'

John grinned. 'Old Arthur.' He slowly shook his head. 'I've never known anybody so disliked in the trade. It's incredible, but nobody likes him. Mind you,' he went on, poking the stove with a long brass poker, 'it's his own fault. Every time you see him, he has always just bought something fantastic with a big profit in it. And he is always bragging about how much money he is making. Personally, I can't stand the man.'

Brian put his empty cup down on the workbench. 'The thing that gets up my nose with him, is that he is always running people down,' he said quietly. 'Tell me John, what actually happened with Mallory?'

'Well.' John stood up from the stove. 'For a start, he hadn't been paying any stamps. Then the income tax had a go at him and finally the VAT got him and finished him off.'

'That's sad, I think,' the Bantam said slowly.

'Sad, hell.' A grin crossed John's face. 'He deserved everything he got. Personally, I don't think it could have happened to a nicer guy!'

Reluctantly Brian agreed with him. The dealer in question was quite an unsavoury character and though it must be said that in general antique dealers were a decent crowd, Arthur Mallory had been the exception to the rule.

The wind continued to wail around Weighbridge House, and the rain continued to fall. The Bantam leaned over from his chair and threw another log on the slowly diminishing fire, causing a flurry of sparks to fly into the wide chimney. 'Arthur Mallory,' he murmured slowly, the effects of his drinking causing his mind to change tack. 'Silly sod.'

He glanced up at the Victorian oil painting that hung over the fireplace and a wistful expression crossed his face as he recalled Rose, stark naked, trying to persuade him to sell her the painting.

'Yes Rose,' he murmured, 'you very nearly got it, didn't you? You were a very persuasive lady. I wonder what you are doing these days? I wonder who you are conning now. With your beautiful body and winning smile.'

Brian had not seen Rose since the incident of the oil painting because he decided that she was just too pushy. Plus the fact that he had grown tired of her, and her selfish ways.

So he had got involved with Heather, and now that she had

gone, he felt very lonely and very reluctant to start any new relationship. As he sat reminiscing by the light of the fire, the loneliness washed over him like a wave on the seashore.

He stood up from his chair, crossed to the dresser and refilled his glass yet again. 'I know what I'll do,' he said, turning, 'I'll phone Heather.' He walked unsteadily over to the telephone that was sitting on a seventeenth century food cupboard in the corner of the room, and dialled Heather's number.

There was no reply.

'Damn.'

He slammed the phone down in exasperation. 'I'll phone Alice,' he thought. He rang Alice's number.

Again there was no reply.

By this time he was getting quite desperate. He needed to talk to someone. Anyone, just as long as he could get rid of this feeling of being alone.

He phoned Stella's number and heard her soft voice informing him that she was not available at the moment, and would he leave a message?

'Bloody answering machines,' he shouted at the receiver as he banged it down, so hard that he almost knocked it off the cupboard.

Brian slumped dejectedly down in his armchair, and with a large swallow finished the last of his drink. He thought of phoning JC in America, but although he had had a lot to drink, he realised that it would not do his image much good if he phoned in his present state.

'Pull yourself together, old son,' he remonstrated with himself. 'You haven't done too badly so far in the antique business. And you have got a long way to go yet.'

He tried phoning Stella again.

Again the disembodied voice came from the answering machine. Just hearing her voice, albeit a recording, made his pulse race a little faster.

'One day, Stella.' He crossed to the now almost empty whiskey decanter. 'One day you and I will get it together. Of that I am certain.' And he returned to his chair, staggering a little as he did so.

The rain had stopped.

The flickering flames diminished as the log fire reluctantly died down, and the peaceful lounge darkened a little more.

The wind continued to wail plaintively around Weighbridge House, as the Bantam's eyes slowly closed, and his head slumped to his chest.

The empty glass dropped from his lifeless fingers, to fall with a soft thud onto the thick pile carpet.

He didn't feel the room become colder.

He wasn't aware of the old lady in the brown dress standing behind his chair, her arms outstretched protectively, and a smile on her face.

The Bantam slept.

ited in the United Kingdom
Lightning Source UK Ltd.
58UKS00002B/106-129